Solid Foundation Sermon Starters

BOOK OF HEBREWS

Blueprints for 30 messages built upon God's Word

D1263068

James R. Girdwood

STANDARD PUBLISHING

Cincinnati, Ohio

All Scripture quotations, unless otherwise indicated, are taken from the HOLY BIBLE, NEW INTERNATION-
AL VERSION®. NIV®. Copyright © 1973, 1978, 1984 by International Bible Society. Used by permission of
Zondervan Publishing House. All rights reserved.

Cover design by Grannan Graphic Design LTD

Interior design by Robert E. Korth

Edited by Bob Buller
© 1999 by The Standard Publishing Company
All rights reserved.
Printed in the U.S.A.

Solid Foundation is an imprint from
The Standard Publishing Company, Cincinnati, Ohio.
A division of Standex International Corporation.
06 05 04 03 02 01 00 99   5 4 3 2 1

Contents

God's New Covenant

The Book of Hebrews

Purpose: To introduce Hebrews and its central theme—the new covenant.

INTRODUCTION

God brought a wonderful new covenant through Jesus. Because Jesus is so closely linked to the covenant, he is called the "covenant" in Isaiah 42:6 and 49:8. Hebrews cites a number of Old Testament passages to show and explain how Jesus established God's new covenant with all of God's people, Jews and Gentiles alike. If we can understand what Hebrews teaches about the new covenant, we will be well on our way to understanding the book of Hebrews as a whole.

Proposition: God invites all people into relationship with him through the superior covenant established by Jesus.

I. THE NEW COVENANT IS SUPERIOR TO THE OLD COVENANT MEDIATED BY MOSES (HEBREWS 8).

A. According to Hebrews 8, the new covenant is superior to the old one in various ways. To prove this point, the author of Hebrews quotes and explains Jeremiah 31:31-34, where God first revealed his intention to establish a new covenant with his people.

B. Jeremiah 31 teaches that the new covenant will be superior to the old covenant made between God and Israel at Mount Sinai in several key respects: (1) the new covenant will link Israel and Judah again into one; (2) the new covenant will put God's law into the people's minds and hearts—the law will no longer be external to them; (3) in this covenant, everyone from the least to the greatest will know God; and (4) the new covenant will provide for total forgiveness. Old Testament forgiveness still awaited Jesus' coming.

II. JESUS ESTABLISHED THE NEW COVENANT BY OFFERING HIMSELF AS A SACRIFICE FOR SIN (HEBREWS 5–7).

A. Hebrews 5–7 teaches that Jesus is our high priest, superior to the earlier high priests in every way. Hebrews 5:6 and 7:17, 21 quote Psalm 110 to demonstrate the superiority of Jesus' priesthood.

For example, God appointed Jesus with a solemn oath. In addition, Jesus' ministry will never end because he functions by the power of an indestructible life. Like Melchizedek, Jesus stands alone with no predecessor or successor (see Genesis 14:18-20 and Hebrews 7:1-3). Finally, Jesus performs his high priestly work in Heaven, in the very presence of the Father.

B. As a high priest, Jesus also offered a superior sacrifice, his own sinless body (Hebrews 10:5-7; cf. Psalm 40:6-8). Whereas Old Testament sacrifices required animals, Jesus offered himself, the very Son of God. Moreover, Jesus offered himself only once, unlike the endlessly repeated sacrifices of the Old Testament.

C. In sum, Jesus' priestly ministry and sacrifice are superior to those of the old covenant in every way.

III. GOD INVITES US TO ENTER INTO HIS NEW COVENANT WITH ALL PEOPLE (HEBREWS 11, 12).

A. As in the Old Testament (Habakkuk 2:4, which is quoted in Hebrews 10:38), even now God requires faith of those who want to please him. Hebrews 11 offers numerous examples of faith that God accepted and honored.

B. Therefore, whoever wants to enter into God's new covenant must believe in Jesus' completed work and trust his high priestly sacrifice for the sins of the entire world.

C. Hebrews 11 also urges us to persevere to the very end, as numerous others have done. Trials are proofs of God's love, not of his abandonment, for God disciplines us so we will be ready to enter his holiness (Hebrews 12; cf. Proverbs 3:11, 12).

CONCLUSION

One of my friends struggled through chemotherapy to arrest a cancer problem. Courageously she endured the treatment's debilitating side effects. Neighbors helped with meals. Fellow workers helped with some of her work load. During this difficult time she boldly wore a wide assortment of hats—straw, velvet, feathered, even Mickey Mouse. Her hats became her redeeming glory.

Jesus is greater than the prophets (Hebrews 1:1, 2), the angels (1:4-14), and even all of history (1:2, 3). In your weakness, put on your new hat. Put on Christ and what he offers all people in God's new covenant.

You Can't Top This!

Hebrews 1:1-4

Purpose: To display how Jesus dominates God's plan for our salvation.

INTRODUCTION

In the past, God spoke in various ways: by walking together with Adam in the Garden of Eden, by visiting over a meal with Abraham, in Jacob's dream with a ladder reaching to Heaven, by showing Moses the exact pattern for the tabernacle, by speaking to Samuel in a voice that sounded like Eli's, by symbolic actions to Ezekiel, and through an angel to Daniel. All these ways, and many more, conveyed bits and pieces of God's Old Testament revelation.

But now, "in these last days," God has revealed himself more directly and clearly than he ever did "in the past" (Hebrews 1:1, 2). God's full, final revelation came directly through his Son. Jesus was the (final) prophet predicted in Deuteronomy 18:15, but he was more than a prophet. He was God's own Son, the Word (John 1:1, 2), the one who fully disclosed what God is like (John 1:18). All history is thus in its final stage now that Jesus has come, and since Jesus culminates all God's revelation to humans, we must look at who he is and listen to all he has said.

Proposition: Jesus dominates all of salvation history because of who he is and what he does.

I. JESUS FAR SURPASSES ANY OTHER PERSON OR THING (HEBREWS 1:1-3).

A. Jesus is the "heir of all things" (Hebrews 1:2). In other words, all that exists will one day be given to him. Throughout history humans have amassed fortunes, often only to leave them to others who will likewise die (Ecclesiastes 2:18-21). But Jesus will inherit all things on earth and in Heaven from his Father, and he will never die nor bequeath his inheritance to another.

B. Jesus radiates God's glory (Hebrews 1:3). Chrysostom wrote about light "radiating" from a light, much as heat and light would "radiate" from an old potbellied stove. In a similar way, Jesus radiates (carries) God's nature out to us, so we feel his presence.

C. Jesus is seated at the right hand of God (Hebrews 1:3). The right hand is the place of greatest honor and of highest authority. There Jesus sits as both king and high priest. According to Hebrews 8:1, Jesus is our royal high priest. Like Melchizedek, Jesus serves as king and priest at the same time (Hebrews 7:1-3).

II. JESUS' DEEDS FAR SURPASS THOSE OF ANY OTHER PERSON (HEBREWS 1:2-4).

A. Jesus created all that exists (Hebrews 1:2). When we read Genesis 1:1—"In the beginning God created the heavens and the earth"—we usually think of God the Father. But Hebrews 1:2 says that God made the universe "through" Jesus. Likewise, John 1:3 says, "Through him [i.e., through Jesus] all things were made; without him nothing was made that has been made."

We could say that the Father did the planning, while Jesus did the hands-on creating. They worked together, with the Holy Spirit also involved (see the reference to the Spirit in Genesis 1:2).

B. Jesus represents God's very essence to us (Hebrews 1:3). The word translated "representation" was used of a "copy" of a book or a coin as a "copy" of a die. A die presses its exact image into the coin, so the coin shows what the die is like. In the same way, Jesus shows us what God is like. Although we are to imitate God (Ephesians 5:1), we are imperfect copies. Jesus is the "exact representation" so that whoever sees Jesus sees God (John 14:9).

C. Jesus sustains all things by his word (Hebrews 1:3). Colossians 1:17 teaches that Jesus was "before all things, and in him all things hold together." We all know that the same magnetic forces repel, but opposites attract. Thus, in an atom, the negative electrons orbit because the positive nucleus attracts them. So why don't the positive protons fly apart? Some powerful force holds the positive charges together in the center of an atom. Jesus' word is this powerful force.

D. Jesus made purification for our sins (Hebrews 1:3). This certainly points to Jesus' death on the cross and high priestly work in Heaven. Nothing impure can enter Heaven (Revelation 21:27), so Jesus makes us pure to enable us to enter God's presence.

In addition, Jesus shed his blood for us, not only to provide forgiveness for our sins, but also to make us his very own, as numerous passages teach: Matthew 26:28; Acts 20:28; Romans 5:9; Ephesians 2:13; Hebrews 9:14, 22; 10:19; 1 Peter 1:18, 19; 1 John 1:7; Revelation 1:5.

CONCLUSION

Jesus is far greater than all the prophets and priests, saints and sages of the Old Testament. He gave God's final, full message to us. It is important to admire his superiority in every step of our creation and redemption. But do you admire him enough to join him? You can join the One who surpasses all today. Simply place your faith in Jesus, the one who shed his blood on the cross to provide forgiveness for your sins and the sins of the entire world.

Better Than Angels

Hebrews 1:5-14

Purpose: To demonstrate the different ways Jesus is superior to the angels.

INTRODUCTION

In 1998, twenty-eight people ran for the office of sheriff in one county, but after the November election, only one was qualified to serve in that capacity—the one who won the election.

In a similar way, various spiritual forces vie for control of human lives and souls. Today people are especially interested in angels and how they might use these spirit beings to draw closer to God. There are good reasons to admire true angels (as opposed to those who followed Satan in rebellion against God): their purity, power, and speed. But Jesus is far superior to the highest angel, as both the Old and New Testaments demonstrate.

Proposition: Jesus is far superior to all God's angels, so we should honor and serve him as such.

I. JESUS STANDS IN A SPECIAL RELATIONSHIP TO THE FATHER (HEBREWS 1:5, 6).

A. In the first place, the Father is especially proud of Jesus' work (Hebrews 1:5). I have always tried to teach my son to help people, but I wasn't sure how well my instruction was taking root. Then one day I observed him helping his sister with her chores, and I thought, "Today, you have become my son." He had been my son all along, but that day he did something distinctive that made me feel even more "related" to him than ever before.

In a similar way, Jesus came to earth and died on the cross to rescue us from our sin. In so doing, he acted so distinctively like the Father that God proudly exclaimed, "Today I have become your Father" (Hebrews 1:5, quoting Psalm 2:7).

B. All this took place to fulfill what God had promised David in 2 Samuel 7:14. When David offered to build God a house (temple), God promised to build David a house (dynasty). God vowed, "I will be his Father, and he will be my Son" (Hebrews 1:5, quoting 2 Samuel 7:14). As the author of Hebrews notes earlier in the verse, God never said anything like this to any of the angels, so Jesus clearly stands in a position superior to that of the angels, in a special relationship with God the Father.

C. God commanded the angels to worship Jesus (Hebrews 1:6). When Jesus was born, angels worshiped him (Luke 2:13, 14). We must not miss the significance of the "heavenly host" of angels worshiping the newborn king. Only God is worthy of worship, but the angels recognized that Jesus, as God incarnate, deserved their worship, their adoration, and their acclaim.

II. JESUS STANDS IN A SPECIAL RELATIONSHIP TO HUMANS (HEBREWS 1:7-14).

A. Whereas Jesus became a human, God "makes his angels winds" (Hebrews 1:7, quoting Psalm 104:4). Humans are the crown of God's creation (Genesis 1:26-28; Psalm 8:3-8), so it is significant that Jesus joined the human family, not the angel family (Matthew 1; Luke 3; Philippians 2).

According to Hebrews 1:14, angels are sent by God to serve humans, as the ravens fed Elijah (1 Kings 17:1-4). Finally, we will judge the angels; they will not judge us (1 Corinthians 6:1-5). In sum, Jesus' incarnation demonstrates his solidarity with us and both his and our superiority to angels.

B. Jesus will reign over all creation, including his people (Hebrews 1:8, 9; Psalm 45:6, 7). Jesus currently sits on his throne (Acts 2:32, 33), waiting for his Father to subdue all his enemies (Hebrews 1:13, quoting Psalm 110:1). Then Jesus and his people will reign over all things (Ephesians 2:4-7). Angels will not enjoy this privilege.

C. Jesus created the universe, and he will bring it to an end (Hebrews 1:10-12, quoting Psalm 102:25-27). We often think of the Father as the creator, but Hebrews 1:2 and John 1:1-3 indicate otherwise. Jesus created all things, so he alone will bring his creation to an end. When the Bible says that he will "roll them up like a robe," it implies that he who is outside of the universe will act on it as he sees fit. Contrary to what many today believe, the universe will not explode at some future time. Jesus will roll it up. When this universe has outlived its purpose, Jesus will bring it to an end. Only God and those who are his will remain.

CONCLUSION

Jesus is superior to the angels both in his special relationship to the Father and in his unique solidarity with humans. Angels are ministering servants (Hebrews 1:14); he is the Son. Jesus, who created all that there is and who will bring all that exists to its final destiny, will reign forever. Angels, however, are "sent to serve those who will inherit salvation" (Hebrews 1:14).

Are you numbered among that group? If not, then honor and trust Jesus, for he alone is worthy of your faith and your praise. If you are among that group, why not put the angels to work? Choose a person or place, and ask God to send "ministers," both angelic and human, to bring the good news of the gospel where it is needed the most (see Matthew 9:38).

Who Will Win It?

Hebrews 2:1-4

Purpose: To encourage people not to neglect "such a great salvation."

INTRODUCTION

When the Powerball Jackpot rose past $200 million, sales went berserk. Finally thirteen people who had joined forces in a ticket pool won the $285 million pot. Even after taxes there was $7 million for each one. One winner said, "No, we weren't having a pool party. We were just hollering." Who wouldn't feel like a little celebration at such a moment? But with stakes so high, one needs to be sure that all the numbers match.

God has offered us more than 285 million years in his mansion—with unlimited spending money. So how can our seventy to eighty years of struggling here on earth compare to that jackpot?

Proposition: Our salvation in Christ is so great that we dare not neglect it.

I. **THE OLD TESTAMENT CONTAINED GOD'S BINDING WILL FOR HIS PEOPLE, ISRAEL (HEBREWS 2:1, 2).**

A. According to Hebrews 2:2, the Old Testament was revealed through angels. God had spoken the basic commands directly to Moses, but he used angels to communicate the rest. For example, Daniel 10:1-14 reports that an angel informed Daniel that his prayer had been heard. In a similar way, an angel told Mary about Jesus' birth (Luke 1:26-28).

B. Nevertheless, the entire Old Testament was binding (Hebrews 2:2). Exodus 19:5 states, "Now if you obey me fully and keep my covenant, then out of all nations you will be my treasured possession." Likewise, Leviticus 18:4 commands, "You must obey my laws and be careful to follow my decrees. I am the Lord your God." Finally, Moses explains in Deuteronomy 6:25, "And if we are careful to obey all this law . . . that will be our righteousness."

C. Moreover, every violation and disobedience of the Old Testament received its just punishment (Hebrews 2:2). The one who murdered lost his or her life, and the thief had to repay what was stolen plus a penalty.

The famous "eye for an eye" law showed Israel's judges that the punishment should match the offense. Exodus 21:23-25 says, "If there is serious injury, you are to take life for life, eye for eye, tooth for tooth, hand for hand, foot for foot, burn for burn, wound for wound, bruise for bruise." This was not permission for personal revenge but a requirement for judges to determine a fair punishment for every crime.

II. BUT THE STAKES ARE NOW HIGHER THAN THEY HAVE EVER BEEN BEFORE (HEBREWS 2:3, 4).

A. Since Jesus' revelation is superior to that found in the Old Testament, how much worse will it be for those who neglect it? The salvation Jesus provides gives us freedom from sin, guilt, and punishment. It also promises us the gift of the Holy Spirit and a heavenly future with God and Jesus.

B. Ignoring "such a great salvation" not only snubs God but also leaves us with no means of escaping his just punishment (Hebrews 2:3). Romans reminds us that "we will all stand before God's judgment seat" (14:10), while Jesus himself warns us that people "will have to give account on the day of judgment for every careless word they have spoken" (Matthew 12:36).

C. Since God both "announced" and "confirmed" this great salvation, we dare not neglect it. God announced it through the ministry and teaching of Jesus. Those who heard him recognized that he spoke with God's own authority (Mark 1:27). God also confirmed the message through "signs" (focusing on the meaning of Jesus' miracles), "wonders" (emphasizing people's reaction to Jesus' deeds), and "miracles" (pointing to God's power to do the impossible). Even now God confirms the salvation message through the gifts of the Holy Spirit (see Acts 5:12-16; Romans 12:3-8; and 1 Corinthians 12–14).

III. IN LIGHT OF SUCH A GREAT SALVATION, WE MUST RESPOND CAREFULLY (HEBREWS 2:1).

A. On the one hand, we must "pay more careful attention . . . to what we have heard" (Hebrews 2:1). This relates to our hearing of God's message: "Faith comes from hearing the message, and the message is heard through the word of Christ" (Romans 10:17).

B. We must also be careful not to drift away or to ignore God's great salvation in Jesus Christ. Hebrews warns us that we will not escape God's punishment if we drift away from Jesus, like a raft carried along on a dangerous current. We dare not ignore God's revelation and provision of salvation announced and confirmed in Jesus.

CONCLUSION

Police officers report that there are often more automobile accidents after an initial accident has taken place than at any other time. People focus on the first accident and do not pay attention to their own driving. The Old Testament tells us what happened to Israel when they ignored God's prior revelation through angels. Let us learn from (rather than imitate) their example by giving careful and committed attention to God's final revelation in his Son.

Jesus to the Rescue!

Hebrews 2:5-18

Purpose: To learn how Jesus brings many people to Heaven.

PREPARATION

Every year the television airwaves and newspapers are filled with advertisements for the latest blockbuster action rescue movie. Whether the story line involves a last-second rescue from some impending natural disaster or a harrowing deliverance from the clutches of evil terrorists, the movie is virtually guaranteed to generate a huge profit for its makers.

People simply love tales of rescue from danger and doom, which is why the story of God's rescue of humanity from the clutches of death remains so compelling. Our Savior is, without a doubt, the greatest rescue hero of all time. Hebrews 2:5-18 tells us in greater detail why this is so.

Proposition: Jesus rescued many people by doing for humans what they were unable to do for themselves.

I. WE LOST OUR EXALTED ROLE AND ENDANGERED OURSELVES THROUGH SIN (HEBREWS 2:5-8, 14).

A. The very first chapter of Genesis clearly teaches that humans were the highest of God's creation. God created us to rule his world (Genesis 1:28). Psalm 8:4-6, which is quoted in Hebrews 2:6-8, repeats this claim, adding that God crowned us "with glory and honor" (Psalm 8:5; cf. Hebrews 2:7). Indeed, God still plans on subjecting "the world to come," not to angels, but to the height of his creation, to a human (Hebrews 2:5, 8).

B. Yet we do not presently see this promised rule, for we sinned (Genesis 3) and thus fell from our noble state into the pits of death and despair. Humanity is currently held in the grip of death and its awful purveyor, who is none other than the devil (Hebrews 2:14). Thus, God's rescue story begins with his highest creation trapped in a life-threatening situation that they fell into of their own free will.

II. JESUS CAME TO THIS WORLD TO RESCUE HUMANITY FROM DEADLY DANGER (HEBREWS 2:9-15).

A. But Jesus, God's hero par excellence, came into this situation to rescue those who could not save themselves. The "son of man" did for humans what they could not do for themselves.

B. The author of Hebrews notes several traits that qualified Jesus for this job. In the first place, Jesus became fully human in order to physically come alongside the ones he would save (Hebrews 2:9, 14, 15). Jesus did not stand apart from those who needed his help. He actually became one of them. Jesus also "suffered death" on behalf of humanity in order to free others from its terrible grip (Hebrews 2:9, 14, 15). Jesus "tasted" that which threatened humans in order to deliver them from their awful fate.

C. By doing what no other rescuer could or would do—sharing in his people's weaknesses and suffering on behalf of them—Jesus not only perfected himself "through suffering" but made them "holy" members of his own family (Hebrews 2:10, 11). Jesus destroyed the one who held us in his deadly grip (the devil) and transferred us safely into his own glorious family (2:10).

III. THOSE WHO CLING TO JESUS WILL BE RESCUED FROM DEATH AND TAKEN TO GLORY (HEBREWS 2:10).

A. The grand finale of God's rescue story is gripping in more ways than one. In much the same way that people are rescued from danger by holding on to a rope that pulls them to safety, we can escape the pit of death by clinging to Jesus as he takes us safely home. The author of Hebrews notes that Jesus is "bringing many sons to glory" (2:10), which is clearly a reference to Heaven, our ultimate destination. Jesus became one of us to become accessible to us, but that is not the end of the story. Jesus also wants us to become part of his family so we can live together in his heavenly home.

B. We will not be rescued because we talk a certain way, happen to have a certain color of skin, belong to a certain church, or perform certain deeds. Only clinging to Jesus in faith will rescue us from death and enable us to go home to glory. Although we fell from our exalted position through willful sin, Jesus lifts us back up when we trust in him.

CONCLUSION

Surely the human mind could not devise a rescue story to compare with this. God created humans to be at the top of creation, but we foolishly and stubbornly fell by sinning against our Creator. Trapped in the pit of death and held firmly in the grasp of Satan, we had absolutely no hope of ever escaping.

But at the right time, God sent Jesus to our rescue. Setting aside the display of his divine nature, he became one of us. Putting aside any thought of self-preservation, he even suffered death on our behalf. In so doing, he not only perfected himself but also made us holy so that when he returned to his heavenly home, we could go with him to enjoy forever God's glorious presence.

Are you gripped by the fear of death? Do you need to be rescued? Hang on to Jesus, and he will take you safely home.

Jesus Is Greater

Hebrews 3:1-6

Purpose: To show by comparison that Jesus is better than the best of people.

INTRODUCTION

The opening chapters of Hebrews compare Jesus to several important people. In every instance Jesus is shown to be superior. He is, quite simply, the greatest of all time.

Former heavyweight champion Muhammad Ali, who once proclaimed himself to be "the greatest," wrote what is believed to be the shortest poem ever: "Me. Whee!" Jesus, however, does not celebrate his superiority. Rather, he uses it for our benefit. That is why Jesus alone is worthy of our honor, praise, trust, and obedience.

Proposition: Jesus is greater than any spiritual power or human personality.

I. ALTHOUGH HE BECAME HUMAN, JESUS IS GREATER THAN ANY OTHER HUMAN.

A. Jesus is greater than the Old Testament prophets (Hebrews 1:1, 2). God's prophets often evoked awe and wonder for their courageous faith and commitment to speak God's word to sinful people. Elijah, for example, opposed four hundred prophets of Baal on Mount Carmel (1 Kings 18). Micaiah dared to raise a solitary voice against the king, telling Ahab and his "prophets" that Ahab would die in the battle and that Israel would suffer defeat (1 Kings 22). John the Baptist, who was greater than all the earlier prophets (Matthew 11:11), called the religious leaders of his day a "brood of vipers" and challenged them to repent from their sins (Matthew 3:7).

Yet none of these paradigms of faith and courage can compare to Jesus. As John himself recognized, he was not worthy even to carry Jesus' sandals (Matthew 3:11). All the prophets of old merely offered a preamble to God's full and final revelation, which was Jesus Christ himself (Hebrews 1:1, 2).

B. Jesus is also greater than other Old Testament heroes of the faith. Joshua, for example, led Israel into the promised land, the place of rest that God had promised to Abraham's descendants. Yet Israel never experienced the rest they so desperately craved. Only one greater than Joshua could provide that rest; only Jesus would fulfill God's promise (Hebrews 4:8).

Jesus is also greater than Abraham, the father of the Israelite people. When Abraham offered tithes to Melchizedek, the priest-king of Jerusalem, he recognized Melchizedek's superiority to him (Genesis 14:18-20). Yet Hebrews tells us that Jesus is even greater than Melchizedek (7:1-28). Consequently, he must be greater yet than Abraham himself.

C. Jesus is even greater than Moses (Hebrews 3:1-6). No Old Testament character was greater than Moses. He shaped the Israelites into a nation, met face to face with God, and conveyed God's law to a sinful people. When God was angry enough with Israel to destroy them, Moses intervened and convinced God to forgive his fallen people (Numbers 14:10-20). No other person in the Old Testament was more revered by the Israelite people than Moses, who spoke with God as one speaks to a friend.

Yet Jesus is greater than even Moses. Moses served faithfully within God's house, but Jesus, God's own Son, rules over that house. It is no surprise, then, that when Moses and Elijah appeared with Jesus, God told the disciples to obey Jesus (Mark 9:7).

II. BECAUSE HE IS FULLY GOD, JESUS IS GREATER THAN ANY SPIRITUAL POWER.

A. Jesus is greater than the angels in various ways. They are God's servants; he is God's Son (Hebrews 1:5, 14). The angels are commanded to worship; Jesus only receives worship (1:6). Angels obey their master, but Jesus rules over all (1:8, 9, 14). Finally, angels are part of creation; Jesus is the creator of all that exists (1:10-12). In every way, then, Jesus is greater than the angels. He alone is worthy of our worship.

B. Jesus is also superior to and greater than the devil. People sometimes fear the devil and his awful power within this world, but God's Word reminds us that Jesus came to "destroy him who holds the power of death—that is, the devil" (Hebrews 2:14; see also 1 John 3:8). Satan was powerless to lead Jesus to sin (Matthew 4:1-11; Hebrews 4:15) and to keep him in the grave (1 Corinthians 15:3, 4, 54-56). Even now Satan is unable to prevent Jesus from building his church (Matthew 16:18). Jesus truly is the greatest of all time, the only one who is greater than every spiritual power and human personality.

CONCLUSION

If you wanted to win a basketball game, who would you choose for your team—Michael Jordan or any one of us here this morning? Obviously, you would choose the greatest player you could possibly find.

The same principle holds true in the spiritual realm. Jesus clearly is greater than any spiritual power or human personality, so it would be foolish to follow anyone other than him. Yet people do it every day. Some seek angelic visitations, hoping somehow to draw closer to God through the experience. Others, Christians included, focus so much on the teachings or personality of a godly human that they lose sight of the one who is both "the author and perfecter of our faith" (Hebrews 12:2). Since Jesus is greater than all others, let us fix our eyes only on him. Let us give him and him alone the honor and obedience that is due the greatest of all time.

Keep Your Heart Soft

Hebrews 3:7-19

Purpose: To discover how privileged people can fail to reach their spiritual potential.

INTRODUCTION

High school reunions reveal a great deal about how wrong teenage perceptions often are. It takes but a few minutes at such an event to recognize that the "good-looking" kids are aging just as quickly as the rest, that the class clown is struggling with the same serious problems that everyone else has to face, and that the person voted "most likely to succeed" probably hasn't.

The same dynamics can be observed on the pages of Scripture. Saul, for example, bore all the outward signs of a successful monarch, yet he is remembered most for his failures and his inglorious death. The same can be said for the Israelites whom God rescued from slavery in Egypt. Having just experienced God's miraculous deliverance through the Red Sea, they surely would have been voted "most likely to succeed" by the people of their day. Yet they all died in failure, never reaching the land God had promised to them and their children. What happened? How could a people with such potential for spiritual success fail so miserably?

Proposition: Unless we keep our hearts soft before God, we will never experience God's success or rest.

I. ISRAEL MISSED GOD'S REST BECAUSE THEY HARDENED THEIR HEARTS TO HIS WORD (HEBREWS 3:7-11, 16).

A. Hebrews 3:7-19 begins by quoting a portion of Psalm 95, a song of praise and instruction. Notably, the author of Hebrews passes over the first part of the psalm, which worships God for his goodness, and includes only the final warning not to disobey (Hebrews 3:7-11; cf. Psalm 95:7-11). There is a time to praise, and there is a time to listen. Clearly this is one of the latter times.

B. The historical event to which the psalm refers was Israel's complaint against God at places called Meribah and Massah, just a few days after crossing the Red Sea (Exodus 17:1-7). The author of Hebrews translates these two place names with their actual meanings: "rebellion" and "testing." About a year later, the people refused to enter Canaan, preferring the bad report of ten spies over the good report of two spies who trusted God to do what he had said. This is when God sentenced them to forty years in the desert, where everyone twenty and older would die (Numbers 13, 14). The Israelites' rebellion was so continuous that Psalm 95 brings the two incidents together.

C. Hebrews asks, "Who were they who heard and rebelled? Were they not all those Moses led out of Egypt?" (3:16). These people enjoyed tremendous advantages—God's presence, visible manifestations of God's power, and God's provision for their daily needs. Yet advantages do not guarantee success. The Israelites failed miserably and never enjoyed God's success or rest. What can we learn from their example?

II. WE CAN AVOID ISRAEL'S FAILURES BY KEEPING OUR HEARTS SOFT BEFORE GOD (HEBREWS 3:13, 14).

A. We face the same danger that the Israelites faced. It is possible for our hearts to become hard, as theirs did. Thus we are warned not to have sinful, unbelieving hearts. Some people are inclined more toward certain sins, but all are inclined toward some sin. But God has given us the power to choose to obey him. We have the power to reject sin's deceitfulness and to hold tightly to the One who promises us life (Hebrews 3:13, 14).

B. We can also help one another avoid becoming hardhearted. Hebrews 3:13 tells us to "encourage one another." We are not designed by God to live life alone. We need others, and others need us. That is why the image of the church as a body is so appropriate (Romans 12:4, 5; 1 Corinthians 12:12-26). We can and should help the other members of the body remain soft and pliable to God's leading and instruction.

Note also that we are to do this on a "daily" basis. Church today tends to make us nudge one another weekly, not daily, which is better than nothing. But God would have us encourage one another every day, keeping ourselves and others tender before God and his Word.

C. We should also remember what we have come to share in Christ (Hebrews 3:14). Think how diligent we would be if the president of our country or our business asked us to participate in a project of his. Jesus has made us partners with him in this project of spreading faith, of bringing many children to glory (2:10).

D. Finally, we must hold on firmly until the end (Hebrews 3:14). The Israelites started out well, but their disobedience and unbelief disqualified them from enjoying God's rest. Hebrews understands the words "Today . . . do not harden your hearts" to imply that God's rest remains open even now (3:7; cf. 4:1). Thus we would do well to remember King Ahab's words that "One who puts on his armor should not boast like one who takes it off" (1 Kings 20:11). Only those whose hearts are softened by faith will enjoy God's promised rest.

CONCLUSION

Don't be satisfied with being the most likely to succeed. Succeed. Keep your heart soft to God and his will. And as you do, help someone else stay faithful. In so doing, you will begin to enjoy the rest God has promised to those who love and obey him.

Sweet Rest

Hebrews 4:1-11

Purpose: To understand how God has provided a "Sabbath rest" for his people.

INTRODUCTION

Everyone enjoys a vacation, a long weekend, or a day off from the daily grind of work and worry. But such times of rest and relaxation are not only enjoyable, they're also necessary. God has made humans in such a way that we all need, both physically, mentally, and emotionally, times of "focused rest."

That was one of the reasons God instituted the Sabbath in the Old Testament. He knew that humans need time away from daily responsibilities to rest and recharge their energy. But the Sabbath also looked forward to that time in the future when God will give us what our bodies and minds really crave, perfect rest and repose in the presence of our loving God. Hebrews 4:1-11 teaches us what this rest will be like and what we need to do in order to experience it in our lives.

Proposition: Only those who remain faithful to Jesus will experience God's rest.

I. THE OLD TESTAMENT SABBATH PREFIGURED GOD'S FUTURE PERFECT REST (HEBREWS 4:9, 10).

A. The Old Testament Sabbath mirrored God's "rest" after the creation of the world. God created the world in six days, then rested (Genesis 1:1–2:4). To remind his people of this great truth, God instituted the Sabbath, a day at the end of each week in which they were to rest from their labors (Exodus 20:8-11; 31:14-17). Therefore, the concept of rest derives its validity from God and his actions. Just as God rested from his labors, so we also should rest from ours.

B. The Old Testament Sabbath provided a day of rest for the Jews (Exodus 20:9, 10). When people are required to work without a regular period of rest, the quality and quantity of their work suffers. Knowing this, God established the Sabbath to give humans time to rest from their labors (Exodus 35:2) and to enjoy his good gifts (Exodus 16:29). However, just as God continued to maintain his creation even after he had "rested" from his creative activity, so also the Israelites rested from their labors at the end of each week, only to take them up once again after the Sabbath had ended. Our future rest, however, will never end. We will cease once and for all from the labors at which we toil (Hebrews 4:9, 10).

C. The Sabbath was to benefit people, not burden them. Jesus reminds us that "The Sabbath was made for man, not man for the Sabbath" (Mark 2:27). The Pharisees had so elevated the Sabbath day that they lost sight of its original intent: to teach God's people of their need for the rest that only he can provide.

D. In sum, God instituted the Sabbath to teach his people to rest in what only he can do. In a similar way, the rest God promises us is to remind us that we are to trust in only what Jesus can do for us (Hebrews 4:9, 10), which is why the Sabbath command was not included in the new covenant for the church (Colossians 2:16, 17).

II. GOD'S REST IS ONLY FOR THOSE WHO REMAIN FAITHFUL TO HIS SON (HEBREWS 4:1, 2, 6, 11).

A. Our faithfulness is not passive. Hebrews 4:1 exhorts, "Let us be careful that none of you be found to have fallen short of it [God's rest]." Later, Hebrews 4:11 adds, "Let us, therefore, make every effort to enter that rest." In other words, our rest does not entail inactivity on our part but reliance upon God and upon Jesus' sacrifice for our sins.

B. Our need for faith is seen in Israel's need for faithfulness (Hebrews 3:7-19). Hebrews 4:2 explains, "We also have had the gospel preached to us, just as they did." The verse may be misleading. The "gospel" here is a general term for "good news." The Israelites did not have the story of Jesus' death, burial, resurrection, and his subsequent offer of forgiveness. They did have the good news that God would bring them into a wonderful new land flowing with milk and honey. But "the message they heard was of no value to them, because those who heard did not combine it with faith" (4:2).

C. Our faithfulness must continue until death. Hebrews 4:6 notes that "some will enter that rest," which implies that some will not. Hebrews 4:11 warns us "to make every effort to enter that rest, so that no one will fall." In other words, only those who are faithful until death will receive the rest and the crown of life that Jesus offers to all people (Revelation 2:10).

CONCLUSION

God fervently desires to give people rest from the trials and troubles, struggles and sin that have plagued humanity since Adam first sinned. But that rest is not something that we will ever achieve on our own.

The good news is that we can experience a measure of rest today, rest from trying to satisfy God's righteous requirements on our own, by trusting in Jesus, the author and perfecter of our faith. And if we persevere in our faith until the very end, until death, we will enjoy forever the eternal rest that God has prepared for his people in Heaven. Sweet rest is coming. Don't miss God's big vacation!

Our Power Sources

Hebrews 4:12-16

Purpose: To identify the sources of power we as Christians have from God.

INTRODUCTION

Which has greater power, a loud motorcycle or a quiet automobile? I ask that question to make a simple point. Volume is not a reliable indicator of true power. In many cases, the people and things in this world that make the most noise are not the most powerful. Granted, we often think that those around us who speak the loudest or who have the voice of the crowd behind them possess great power, but we dare not forget that God, the most powerful of all, came to Elijah in "a gentle whisper" (1 Kings 19:12).

God's power is not like that of the world. He can thunder from the heavens when he chooses (Psalm 29:3-11), but often God prefers to work quietly through the lives of those he calls his own. Hebrews 4:12-16 lists several of God's powerful resources, power sources he has given to us to make a mighty difference in our world.

Proposition: God works quietly but powerfully through his Word, our Lord, and our prayers.

I. GOD'S WORD IS A POWERFUL RESOURCE THAT CHANGES PEOPLE'S LIVES (HEBREWS 4:12, 13).

A. Because the Bible penetrates the joints and marrow, it has the power to produce perspective and insight. I love to teach young people Psalm 119:99, 100: "I have more insight than all my teachers, for I meditate on your statutes. I have more understanding than the elders, for I obey your precepts." God's powerful Word gives us insight into our needs and God's will for our lives.

B. The Bible has the power to uncover people's thoughts and attitudes and, if necessary, convict of sin. Since the Bible was produced under the Spirit's guidance, it is not surprising that it has his power to convict (see John 16:7-11). Humans are able to judge only actions, but God can judge motives and inner "secret" thoughts. Hebrews 4:13 says, "Nothing in all creation is hidden from God's sight. Everything is uncovered and laid bare before the eyes of him to whom we must give account."

C. Because the Bible is a living book, it has the power to produce faith. Dwight L. Moody once remarked, "I prayed for faith and thought that some day faith would come down and strike me like lightning. But faith never seemed to come. Then one day I read in Romans 10, 'Now faith cometh by hearing, and hearing by the word of God.' I had closed my Bible and prayed for faith. I now opened my Bible and began to study, and faith has been growing ever since." God uses his quietly powerful Word to give us insight into our situations, to convict us of any sin, and, as a result, to produce a pure faith that will serve as a powerful testimony to those around us.

II. WE SERVE A POWERFUL LORD WHO PROVIDES ALL THAT WE NEED TO LIVE FOR GOD (HEBREWS 4:14, 15).

A. Jesus was not only a high priest but also a "great" high priest (Hebrews 4:14). It is almost a redundancy, but it points out Jesus' superiority to every other high priest who ever served. Jesus' supremacy reflects the excellence of his ministry, which is offered in the very presence of God by the Son of God.

B. Jesus was also tempted in every way, just as we are, yet remained without sin (Hebrews 4:15). In a sense, we do not know how difficult temptation can be because we give in before the temptation reaches its strongest point. Jesus never collapsed. In addition, although Jesus was not tempted in all the specific ways we are, he did face the different *kinds* of temptations that humans face. His rejection of every temptation offers us an example to follow.

C. As a result, Jesus is able to sympathize with our weaknesses. Philippians 2:5-11 reminds us that Jesus' greatest act of power was his conscious decision to give up the trappings of glory that he enjoyed in Heaven to take on the form of a servant, perhaps the weakest class in the ancient world. Later Hebrews 5:8 informs us that Jesus did this to learn "obedience from what he suffered." Jesus, the very Son of God, suffered in order to show us how God can use our weaknesses as a backdrop against which to display his even greater power.

III. GOD OFFERS US THE POWERFUL PRIVILEGE OF PRAYER TO OUR POWERFUL LORD (HEBREWS 4:16).

A. God not only allows us but urges us to approach him in prayer. Because of Jesus' work on the cross, we can approach God boldly, with confidence that our prayers will be heard.

B. Such confidence is based, not on our own worthiness, but on the promise of God's Word that we will "receive mercy and find grace to help us in our time of need" (Hebrews 4:16). We as humans are weak and inadequate, but God's Word and our Lord invite us to tap into God's power through prayer. We will never be more powerful than when we kneel before our Father in prayer.

CONCLUSION

In a world consumed with power, Christians must remember that God's ways are not human ways, that God empowers us to serve him through his Word, our Lord, and our prayers. Spend time each day tapping into God's power sources.

Right for the Job!

Hebrews 5:1-10

Purpose: To learn how Jesus is better for the job than any other priest.

INTRODUCTION

Common to most religions is the notion that only certain people are qualified to approach a holy God. One sees this dynamic in the Old Testament, where only members of the tribe of Levi were authorized to offer sacrifices to atone for the people's sins. In addition, only one priest, the high priest, could enter God's presence in the Holy of Holies, and this only once a year. In short, access to God was limited and depended on the intercession of another person.

We see a similar phenomenon in some churches today. Christians often feel that they cannot approach God directly, that a pastor or other church leader must represent them before God. When they have needs, they ask the pastor to pray for them. When they need spiritual guidance, they ask a church leader what God would have them do. In a sense, this is as it should be. God is holy and we are sinful, so we need someone to represent us before him. Still, one must ask, what qualifies someone to serve as a "priest," to represent God's people before God?

Proposition: Jesus' superior high priestly ministry allows us to enter God's presence daily, freely, and confidently.

I. OUR REPRESENTATIVES MUST HAVE A HUMAN ORIGIN AND A DIVINE APPOINTMENT (HEBREWS 5:1-4).

A. According to Hebrews 5:1, Old Testament high priests were "selected from among men . . . to represent them in matters related to God." The human origin of the priests enabled them to offer concrete gifts and sacrifices on behalf of the Israelites. They bridged the physical world with the spiritual by helping worshipers express faith (an intangible) in tangible ways.

B. In addition, the priests, being human and weak themselves, were able to deal gently with the spiritually "ignorant" who were easily led into sin (Hebrews 5:2). Unlike King Rehoboam, who responded roughly to the people under his care (1 Kings 12:13), the priests were to nurture and help the weak among them, admitting that they themselves were sinful and needed God's forgiveness.

C. Finally, the priests served only because of a divine appointment (Hebrews 5:4). In fact, the priests were not spiritually superior to the rest of the people. The priests had to offer sacrifices for their own sins before they did likewise for the sins of the people. The priests' position was not earned by merit but based only on God's gracious and sovereign appointment.

II. JESUS MET AND SURPASSED ALL THE REQUIREMENTS GOD'S REPRESENTATIVES MUST HAVE (HEBREWS 5:4-10).

A. Jesus was appointed by God to be high priest, just as Aaron was (Hebrews 5:4, 5). The author of Hebrews cites Psalm 2:7 to show that Jesus possessed a superior status, namely, that of being God's Son. In addition, God promised Jesus a unique priesthood that far surpassed the Levitical one (Hebrews 5:6; cf. Psalm 110:4). Therefore, Jesus' high priestly ministry is far superior to any other ministry in terms of its divine origin and credentials.

B. Jesus also became fully human, so he is fully qualified to sympathize with and represent other humans. Hebrews 5:7 reminds us that, while Jesus was on earth, he offered up "prayers and petitions." Some of these prayers were for himself, to be sure, but Jesus also prayed for others (see Matthew 23:37; Luke 22:31, 32; John 17:1-26). His intercession for us with the Father demonstrates the type of love that a true representative must have.

C. Finally, Jesus, who was without sin, still "learned obedience" by submitting himself to suffering on our behalf. Submission involves obeying another's decision and judgment when ours is different, and it is one of the hardest lessons to learn. As a result of his submission, Jesus' prayers were heard by the Father (Hebrews 5:7), and he was "made perfect" (5:9).

We think of "perfection" as "flawlessness," so "to be made perfect" is to have flaws removed. But in the Bible "perfection" is completeness or maturity, so to "be made perfect" is to finish a task or to achieve completeness. Jesus, by his death and resurrection, completed the task the Father had set before him, and by his one sacrifice made us perfect (Hebrews 10:14). Whereas the Old Testament priests could only offer tentative forgiveness as they waited for the Messiah to come, Jesus was both God's Son and Messiah, and he, the source of eternal salvation, offers us full and final forgiveness. In sum, Jesus represents us before God in a way no other person could.

CONCLUSION

Even today Christians often feel as though they need a human representative to take their prayer requests to God and to guide them in God's will for their lives. But such an attitude runs the risk of diminishing Jesus' superior representation of us to God. Christians do need one another for support, encouragement, and guidance, but no other person can truly represent us before God. That is a job only Jesus can fill.

Only Jesus fulfilled and even surpassed the requirements that God set forth for his representatives. Only Jesus can provide eternal salvation and genuine intercession for God's people. So don't settle for second best. Go to the man who is right for the job for whatever needs you might have. Go to Jesus alone, for he alone can represent you effectively before the Father.

The Basics and Beyond

Hebrews 6:1-3

Purpose: To identify and understand the basics of our Christian faith.

INTRODUCTION

Anyone who has ever been involved in a construction project knows the importance of a solid foundation. For example, a while back, a new bridge was being built across the Ohio River a few miles upstream from Cincinnati. A structure of this size and weight would require a solid footing, so the construction workers not only dug down to solid rock but also drilled ten feet into the rock to ensure that the bridge would have a sound base on which to rest. Only then did the workers begin to erect the bridge itself.

The process of building one's faith bears a striking similarity to building a bridge or any other structure. One must begin with a solid foundation or risk the collapse of the entire edifice. Fortunately, God's Word provides all that we need to establish the foundation of our faith. Hebrews 6:1-3 identifies some of the key elements that must form a part of that foundation.

> **Proposition:** We need to understand the basis of our faith
> so we can go on to Christian maturity and service.

I. OUR CHRISTIAN FAITH MUST BEGIN WITH REPENTANCE AND FAITH (HEBREWS 6:1).

A. Repentance is a change of mind that leads to a change of life. It is much like an about-face in marching. Before repentance, we were going our own way, but after repentance we go God's way. To use another analogy, repentance is like turning a steering wheel. It requires a great deal of turning to manuever out of a driveway and onto a street, much less to stay on the road. In a similar way, our initial (large) act of repentance brings us to God, while repeated (small) acts of repentance keep us there.

B. According to Hebrews 6:1, we must all repent "from acts that lead to death," from sinful acts that both anger and sadden God. The Bible says that "there is a way that seems right to a man, but in the end it leads to death" (Proverbs 14:12 and 16:25). In short, faith has no foundation until a person turns from both the attitudes and actions that separate him or her from God.

C. Every time the Bible places repentance and faith side by side, repentance comes first (Matthew 21:32; Mark 1:15; Acts 19:4; 20:21; Hebrews 6:1).

Evidently we must first turn to God before we can trust him. Changing to God's way comes before clinging to his person, but you cannot have one without the other. True faith is founded on repentance that leads to faith.

II. GOD ENABLES US FOR SERVICE THROUGH BAPTISMS AND LAYING ON HANDS (HEBREWS 6:2).

A. The New Testament refers to a number of different "baptisms" that believers undergo. For example, *we* are to be baptized with water (Matthew 28:19, 20; Acts 2:38), while *God* promises to baptize us with the Holy Spirit (Matthew 3:11, 12; Acts 1:5). While the former symbolizes God's purification of those who trust in his Son, the latter enables Christians to serve God and others. The fact that the plural "baptisms" is used here may indicate that the original readers of Hebrews were arguing about the various forms of baptism that were current in that day. They may have forgotten, as we dare not, that baptism both symbolizes and effects a change in a person's life, a change that is epitomized in service to God and others.

B. "Laying on of hands," though unusual these days, was a common means of setting aside someone for service. In the early church, it officially assigned people to a specific task (Acts 6:1-6; 13:1-3; 1 Timothy 5:22) or gave them the power to perform miracles (Acts 8:14-19; 2 Timothy 1:6). As before, however, the emphasis was on building on one's foundational faith by serving others.

III. WE LOOK FORWARD TO A FUTURE DAY OF RESURRECTION AND JUDGMENT (HEBREWS 6:2).

A. We are motivated to build on our foundation because of two future certainties: the resurrection of the dead and the final judgment (Hebrews 6:2). Since the word "dead" here is plural, it does not refer simply to Jesus. Rather, both the righteous and the wicked will be raised to life at the end of this present age (John 5:21-29; Acts 24:15).

B. For those who have placed their faith in Christ, the resurrection will begin a time of unimaginable blessing (Matthew 25:34; 2 Corinthians 4:13–5:21). On the other hand, the wicked will be raised only to be judged (Mark 9:42-48). In either case, judgment is unavoidable, just, and permanent, for "man is destined to die once, and after that to face judgment" (Hebrews 9:27). Knowing this, we should make sure that our foundation is secure, resting on nothing else than a pure and persevering faith in Jesus.

CONCLUSION

Our faith will only be as strong as its foundation, but we must not miss the overriding point of these few verses in Hebrews. As important as a solid foundation may be, it is of no value if we never build anything on it. Therefore, let us not only make sure that our foundation is secure but also build an active and serving faith that will continue to grow until God's time for us on earth has come to an end.

The Most Tragic Error

Hebrews 6:4-12

Purpose: To understand how far we fall if we ever leave Christ.

INTRODUCTION

Even a quick glance at a daily newspaper will reveal just how much tragedy there is in this world. One day we read of the death of a child or a young adult in the prime of life, while the next we are forced to ponder the plight of refugees in some war-torn nation half a world away. Every day we read multiple accounts of murder and assault, and all too often the perpetrators of these crimes are kids who have yet to reach their eighteenth birthday.

There is no escape from these types of tragedy. We can only hope that they do not invade our own private worlds, that they do not touch ourselves or those whom we love. Yet there is a far greater tragedy that any of us could face, a tragedy that often falls on those in the church. Fortunately, it is a tragedy that can be avoided. Today's passage tells us how to protect ourselves from its insidious grip.

Proposition: People who fall away from Christ
will experience the most tragic loss of all.

I. GOD GIVES HIS PEOPLE TREMENDOUS PRIVILEGES AND POSSIBILITIES (HEBREWS 6:4, 5).

A. The author of this passage uses several phrases to describe the privileges of becoming a Christian. For example, Hebrews 6:4 states that they have "once been enlightened." It is as though a thick veil blocking people's vision, a veil that kept them from seeing their own sin and God's free offer of forgiveness, has been removed (2 Corinthians 3:14). The use of the word "once" may be significant. Just as the high priest entered the holiest place only once a year and Jesus died only once for our sins (Hebrews 9:7, 26-28), it may be that the unveiling takes place only once in a person's life. What a tragedy to ignore or reject God's enlightening of our souls.

B. Christians have also "tasted the heavenly gift" (Hebrews 6:4). Tasting speaks of partaking or coming to know something, of experiencing, though possibly in a limited manner, the essence of some good thing. It parallels the idea of "sharing" in something, in this case, the Holy Spirit. God sent his Holy Spirit to enable Christians to preach the good news and to perform mighty deeds in the name of Jesus. The presence of the Spirit testifies to the fact that God has made us his vital partners in the gospel mission. For example, although

27

the Holy Spirit brought Philip to the Ethiopian official, God allowed Philip to tell the gospel story (Acts 8:26-40).

C. Finally, Christians have also "tasted the . . . word of God and the powers of the coming age" (Hebrews 6:5). God's Spirit gives us a foretaste of what the coming kingdom will be like. We experience, though only partially, the powers and the privileges that will only come fully when Christ returns.

II. THOSE WHO FALL AWAY FROM CHRIST WILL EXPERIENCE A TRAGIC LOSS (HEBREWS 6:4-6).

A. The author of this passage also uses several phrases to describe those who leave Christ. In the first place the word "if" and the phrase "because to their loss" are interpretive comments added by the translators (Hebrews 6:6). One could translate this verse, "while they are falling away . . . and crucifying." If this is the actual meaning, then the author is not speaking of a single, permanent event but an ongoing condition, continued rejection of Jesus' sacrifice for their sins on the cross.

B. When this "falling away" takes place, "it is impossible . . . to be brought back to repentance" (Hebrews 6:4, 6). This statement should cause us to tremble. Those who continue to "crucify" Christ, "subjecting him to public disgrace," cannot be restored. They have rejected the only means for a right relationship with God. They have refused their only hope. They have suffered the most tragic loss of all, the loss of their very souls.

III. ANYONE CAN AVOID FALLING AWAY FROM CHRIST AND SUFFERING SUCH LOSS (HEBREWS 6:7-12).

A. Christians are not only to hold fast to the foundations of the faith (Hebrews 6:1-3), but also to go on to maturity (6:11-14). To use the analogy of this passage, we must continually grow so we produce a "crop" that is pleasing and acceptable to God (6:7, 8). Salvation is always proven by its works, and God will both enable us to do and reward us for acts of service to him (6:9, 10).

B. We must also hold on persistently to faith and hope until the end (Hebrews 6:11, 12). Planting a seed achieves nothing if the seed dies before it produces a crop. So it is with the promise of God's salvation. It is not enough to plant the seed of God's Word. We must also nurture that seed until it produces the crop of an unfailing faith and hope in our lives.

CONCLUSION

The good news that God has provided everything we need for salvation leads to both wonderful blessing and the potential for error. Let us not become "lazy" with respect to our salvation. God offers us great privileges, but they come with a great responsibility. Let us make sure that we never fall away from Christ and thus suffer the most tragic loss anyone can ever experience.

Do You Promise?

Hebrews 6:13-20

Purpose: To discover and appreciate the certainty of God's promises.

INTRODUCTION

Sooner or later everyone experiences the hurt of a promise broken or the guilt of a commitment that was not kept. Perhaps a parent failed to attend an important game or school function, or maybe a spouse broke the vow "till death do us part." The stories may vary, but the experience is common.

That is why we require notaries to witness contracts and courtroom witnesses to take an oath. We know that people often break the promises and commitments that they make, so we do what we can to force people to be true, threatening them with punishment if they are not. Remarkably enough, although God's very nature is truth (John 14:6), he has condescended to our ways, taking an oath to make his promises seem even more sure. Such an act reveals not only the trustworthiness of his word but also the great love he has for us, his untrustworthy servants.

Proposition: The promises of God are sure because the one who made them is truth himself.

I. GOD'S VERY NATURE IS TRUTH, SO WHATEVER HE PROMISES IS SURE (HEBREWS 6:13).

A. Hebrews 6:18 states that God guaranteed his promise to Abraham "by two unchangeable things." In context, the one is clearly God's oath. The other is merely implied here but evident throughout all of Scripture, namely, God's own character.

B. For example, James 1:17 says that God "does not change like shifting shadows," while Number 23:19 states, "God is not a man, that he should lie, nor a son of man, that he should change his mind." God is immutable, so whatever he promises is certain to take place. As Hebrews explains, "since there was no one greater for him to swear by, he swore by himself" (6:13). Because God's very nature does not change, his promises will not change or falter.

II. GOD ALSO GUARANTEES HIS PROMISES THROUGH A SURE OATH (HEBREWS 6:13-17).

A. The immutability of God's character ensures the certainty of his promises, but God did not stop here. Recognizing that humans need something tangible to grasp, God stooped to our level and confirmed his promise by taking an oath. No one forced God to do this, and no one could argue if he simply told us to take him at his word. But in order to show us his commitment to his word and his great love for us, God "swore by himself" to make it easier for us to believe in him.

B. An oath not only confirms what is said (Hebrews 6:16) but also puts an end to argument by making one's intentions clear (6:16, 17). That God swore by two unchangeable things (6:18) is in keeping with Old Testament law, which required the testimony of two witnesses in a capital matter (Deuteronomy 19:15). Thus we can confidently trust in God's promises. Not only was God's promise to Abraham proven true (Hebrews 6:13-15), but God's promises to us are also guaranteed because of God's character and his solemn oath.

III. GOD HAS PROMISED TO BLESS HIS PEOPLE IN A VARIETY OF WAYS (HEBREWS 6:14, 15).

A. God had promised "many descendants" to Abraham when he was already seventy-five, and Abraham had to wait another twenty-five years to see the promise begin to be fulfilled (Hebrews 6:14, 15; Genesis 12:1-4; 21:1-5). But by the time Hebrews was written, there was no doubt that God had indeed kept his word to make of Abraham a great nation.

B. God has also made many promises to us, and we can rest confidently in the certainty of those promises even when it seems that they are not yet being fulfilled. For example, God has promised . . .
never again to destroy all living creatures (Genesis 8:21).
to bless all nations through Abraham and his seed, Jesus (Genesis 12:3).
to give rest to every soul and forgive every sin (Matthew 11:28-30; 12:31).
to be with us always, to the end of the age (Matthew 28:20).
to prepare a place for us where we can be with him always (John 14:1-3).
to give us the Holy Spirit to help us spread the good news (Acts 1:8).
to supply all our needs through Christ Jesus his Son (Philippians 4:19).
to keep us from falling so we can enjoy eternal life with God (Jude 24).

CONCLUSION

A human analogy should remind us that we have every reason to believe that God will do exactly what he has promised to do. After a long wait in the courtroom, the jurors are finally selected. Attorneys examine them and remove any who might have a problem being impartial. Finally the trial begins. In an impressive ceremony the judge asks each witness to raise a right hand and take an oath pledging to be completely truthful. Although our obligation to be honest does not depend on that oath, there is something about that ceremony that puts a bit more solemnity in the commitment to the truth. In a similar way, God, whose very nature is truth, took an oath to confirm his promises to us! How, then, could we ever doubt that he will keep his promises in his perfect way and his perfect time?

Jesus Has a Better Way

Hebrews 7:1-28

Purpose: To see how Jesus' approach is better than any other approach to God.

INTRODUCTION

In all likelihood, most of us have vivid memories of choosing up sides for a children's game. For some, those memories are pleasant because they were generally chosen first on account of their athletic or intellectual skill. For most of us, however, the memory of choosing up sides carries with it feelings of disappointment or even embarrassment. We were never chosen first, and sometimes we stood on the sidelines watching as everyone else enjoyed the "honor" of being selected for the team.

As painful as these memories might be, they reveal an important truth. Whether choosing up sides for children's games or adult tasks, we want the best players on our team. In the same way, when we choose someone to represent us before God, we want the best. According to Hebrews 7:1-28, we should want only Jesus.

Proposition: Jesus' approach to God is better than any other approach.

I. JESUS IS BETTER THAN MELCHIZEDEK (HEBREWS 7:1-10).

A. Genesis 14 provides us background information about Melchizedek. A priest of God Most High, his name means "king of righteousness." He ruled Salem (later called Jerusalem), which means "peace"—so he is also "king of peace." By way of contrast, Jesus is called "The LORD our righteousness" (Jeremiah 23:6; 33:16) and "Prince of Peace" (Isaiah 9:6, 7). See also Ephesians 2:11-18, where Jesus reconciles far and near into one.

B. Melchizedek's importance is seen in his receiving tithes from Abraham (7:4-6, 8-10). The superior person received tithes; thus Melchizedek was greater than even Abraham. Later in Israel's history, the tithe was collected by Levites who, like all humans, died (7:8-10). Jesus, on the other hand, was exempt from the normal fees for Jews (Matthew 17:24-27).

C. Melchizedek's importance is seen in his blessing Abraham (7:7-10). Hebrews 7:7 states: "And without doubt the lesser person is blessed by the greater." Since Melchizedek blessed Abraham, Melchizedek is greater. Since, however, Jesus pronounced blessings on many people (Matthew 5:3-12; 11:6; 13:16; 16:17), he is superior to Melchizedek.

II. JESUS IS BETTER THAN AARON (HEBREWS 7:11-28).

A. The Levitical priests could not attain perfection (7:11). If the Levitical priest-hood were adequate, there would have been no need for another priest, a single priest like Melchizedek (or Jesus). Also, the law made nothing perfect, so a better hope by which we draw near to God was introduced (7:19). This "hope" is not a wish, like a lottery ticket, but an expectation, like a paycheck. As such, this better hope is an anchor for our souls (6:19).

Hebrews 7:12 seems to be stated backwards. One would expect it to say that the change of law would require a change of priesthood; instead, changing the priesthood required changing the law. To understand this, we must recall that Jesus was such a dominant person that when he appeared on the scene everything had to change to fit around who he was.

B. By Old Testament law only Aaron's descendants could be priests. The rest of the tribe of Levi could assist them (Exodus 28, 29; Numbers 18:20-24). This partly explains the terrible punishment of Nadab and Abihu, who disobeyed God immediately upon being ordained as priests (Leviticus 8–10).

Unlike the Old Testament priests, who were "sons of Aaron"—a very nar-row group—Jesus was "the Son of Man," embracing the whole human fami-ly. See Matthew 8:20; 9:6; 10:23; 11:19.

C. Aaron was 123 years old when he died (Numbers 33:39). Josephus says there were eighty-three high priests (*Antiquities* XX:224 (XX.20.1ff.), all of whom died. But Jesus overcame death because it was impossible for death to hold him (Acts 2:24). Therefore, he lives forever (7:24), and all who believe in him cross over from death to life (John 5:24; 8:51).

D. Old Testament priests entered their office without an oath (7:20), but Jesus entered his office of priest with an oath of God (7:20, 21). The certainty of God's promise was assured by an oath (6:13-20). The certainty of Jesus' priesthood is also assured by an oath. Hebrews often quotes Psalm 110:4 (5:6, 10; 6:20; 7:11, 17, 21). This oath assures us that Jesus brought a better covenant (7:22).

Illustration: Good companies stand behind their products. Best of all is a money-back guarantee if you are dissatisfied for any reason. I have a friend who bought a computer with a wonderful three-year guarantee. When he had a problem about a year later, the company was no longer in business. Contrast this with what I read of a Rolls Royce customer who had a major car problem. He called the toll-free Rolls Royce dealer, and they immediately flew a repairman with the part to his location. When no bill came for the work, he phoned the company to inquire. They said there was no charge.

CONCLUSION

Jesus' way is better because he meets our needs by his character (7:26), by his sacrifice (7:27), and by his permanence (7:28). There is no one else more qualified to represent us before God. There is no one better to choose for your team.

This One Is Better

Hebrews 8:6

Purpose: To discover ways Christianity is better than any other religion.

INTRODUCTION

We live in a time in which tolerance reigns supreme. We are expected to accept not only other people regardless of their character and actions but also other worldviews no matter what they might be. It is not unusual to hear people today argue that there is no such thing as absolute truth, to claim that all religious beliefs are equally valid if the one who holds them is sincere in his or her commitment to them.

It is difficult to know how to respond in such an intellectual climate. Granted, we are to accept others as God has accepted them, but we should not remain silent in the face of the claim that all religions are equally valid. The book of Hebrews offers compelling reasons why Christianity is superior to all other religions (see 1:4; 7:22; 8:6; 9:23; 11:4), so, like the author of Hebrews, we should be ready to point out just how superior our Lord actually is.

Proposition: Jesus offers us a better ministry, a better covenant, and better promises than any other religious figure.

I. JESUS HAS A BETTER MINISTRY THAN ANY OTHER PERSON.

A. Hebrews 8:6 states matter-of-factly that Jesus has received a better ministry, obviously from the Father, than any other person. In context, Jesus' ministry is being compared with those of Moses and Israel's high priests. Since both ministries derived from God, one might ask why Jesus' ministry is so much better.

B. In the first place, Jesus ministers in Heaven, not on earth. Jesus is currently reigning in Heaven, where he intercedes for us (Acts 2:29-36; Hebrews 7:25). In addition, Jesus' ministry leads us to Heaven (2:10) so we can experience and enjoy God's glorious presence for all eternity.

C. Jesus' ministry is also superior because of what it accomplishes. Jesus offers us full and final forgiveness (Hebrews 8:12; see Matthew 6:12-15; Acts 2:38) so we cannot only overcome the fear of death but also death itself (Hebrews 2:14). Finally, Jesus also gives us help in our time of need (4:16). No one else can offer the type of ministry that Jesus does. No other "religion" compares with Christianity, which is based on Jesus' works and words.

II. JESUS ESTABLISHED A BETTER COVENANT BETWEEN GOD AND HUMANS.

A. As before, Hebrews compares Jesus' work to the Jewish religion set forth in the Old Testament. The mere fact that Jesus established a "new" covenant implies that something was wrong with the old, much as a new edition of a book includes corrections and improvements of the old.

B. Specifically, Jesus' covenant has a better high priest, a better system of sacrifice, and a better provision for godly living. Before Jesus, only some people had God's Spirit, and then only for limited times of special service. But now all believers are indwelt by the Spirit, so all are enabled to live in a way that pleases God (Acts 2:38; Galatians 5:22, 23). Most religions attempt to devise some sort of covenant or contract between the human and the divine, but only Jesus offers a perfect covenant that ensures a harmonious relationship between God and his people.

III. JESUS OFFERS BETTER PROMISES TO THOSE WHO TRUST IN HIS NAME.

A. The old covenant promises of land, family, and blessings focused primarily on Israel, with everyone else participating in an indirect way (Genesis 12:1-3). Moreover, the Old Testament covenant was broken by Israel's unfaithfulness on more than one occasion (Joshua 7:11, 15; Judges 2:20; 1 Kings 19:10; 2 Kings 17:15; 18:12; Psalm 78:10; Jeremiah 11:8; 22:9; Ezekiel 16:59; 17:18, 19; Hosea 6:7; 8:1; Malachi 2:10), so Israel did not experience what God had promised.

B. Jesus' new covenant promises, however, are offered to all, regardless of race (Galatians 3:28). In addition, these promises are guaranteed by *Jesus'* faithfulness (Jude 24), so they are certain for all who trust in him. Unlike the old covenant promises, which focused on this world, Jesus promises us a kingdom not of this world (John 18:36), a spiritual family of great size (Matthew 19:29), and the spiritual blessing of eternal life (John 3:3-5; 10:10). Although others may make similar promises, no one else can produce the results that Jesus produces.

CONCLUSION

As always, there is no shortage of religions claiming to offer a better way to spiritual growth and ultimate happiness. But Christianity is the only "religion" that can both promise and produce what the human heart longs for. Only Christianity offers a genuine relationship with God through the superior ministry of his Son, Jesus. So we must not be silent when those around us claim that Christianity is no better or worse than other religions. Nothing could be further from the truth, and, like the author of Hebrews, we must stand boldly for the truth.

But if you have not yet found true religion, accept no substitutes. Place your faith in Jesus, who is better than any religion in every way.

Sign on the Dotted Line

Hebrews 8:7-13

Purpose: To show how the new covenant exceeds the old.

INTRODUCTION

No doubt we have all purchased something by contract. Perhaps you remember a recent house closing or signing the contract to buy your first car. Contracts are useful, for they specify to everyone involved just what is required of each party. They enable us to enjoy the benefits of whatever we purchase because we know exactly what it will cost us and precisely what we are to get.

As odd as it may sound to some, Christians also have a contract with God. In his grace, God stoops to our level of understanding and promises us certain benefits if we agree to the terms of his offer. This really shouldn't surprise us, for God also had a covenant with Israel. But the contract he has made with us far surpasses the one he made with Israel.

Proposition: The new covenant established by Jesus surpasses the old in terms of its effectiveness, its breadth, and its benefits.

I. JESUS ESTABLISHED A NEW COVENANT BECAUSE THE OLD ONE HAD FAILED (HEBREWS 8:7-10).

A. God promised to make a new covenant (Hebrews 8:8-10; cf. Jeremiah 31:31-34) to correct a weakness in the old one with Israel. The weakness of the old covenant is seen in several ways. God said that he had taken Israel "by the hand to lead them out of Egypt" (Hebrews 8:9). This is terminology one generally associates with a little child, which is not bad in and of itself, but it appears that Israel never progressed beyond "spiritual infancy" in their relationship with God. Evidence of this is seen in the fact that the Israelites "did not remain faithful to" God's covenant.

B. Because Israel broke the covenant, God "turned away from them" (Hebrews 8:9). The failure was not so much in the covenant as it was in the people, but the result was the same. God's contract with Israel was forever broken. It is much like the repossession of a car or furniture. If the buyer does not keep up the payments, he or she loses the benefits and the contract is considered broken. The new covenant, however, is eternal. Because it is based on Jesus' finished work on the cross, it cannot be broken. It is, then, vastly superior to the old covenant in terms of its effectiveness and its endurance.

II. JESUS OFFERS THE NEW COVENANT TO ALL PEOPLE, NOT JUST ISRAEL (HEBREWS 8:9).

A. Although one might understand Hebrews 8:9 to indicate that the new covenant will be made just with Israel, several considerations argue otherwise. First, the phrase "house of Israel . . . and house of Judah" served, in Jeremiah's day, to designate all of God's people and not just the members of a particular group. Moreover, the New Testament clearly teaches that the new covenant is for all who believe regardless of their nationality (Galatians 3:26-29).

B. Whereas participation in the old covenant was based on birth, inclusion in the new covenant is based on faith. All believers, all Jews and Gentiles who trust in Jesus, are included in this new covenant. Thus, the new covenant is superior to the old one because it includes more people within its terms.

III. THE BENEFITS OF THE NEW COVENANT ARE SPIRITUAL, NOT MERELY PHYSICAL (HEBREWS 8:10-13).

A. The benefits of the old covenant were mainly physical: a secure land, many descendants, and divine blessing (Genesis 12:1-3; 28:1-14). There is nothing wrong with these types of benefits, but they pale in comparison with those promised under the new covenant.

B. For example, God pledges to give his new covenant partners new hearts and minds to obey his will (Hebrews 8:10). God's "law" will no longer be external to his people but an internal reality inscribed on their hearts. Moreover, God establishes a personal relationship with his people (8:10). Contracts may, at times, depersonalize relationships between the two parties, but not so here. God's new covenant provides the means for God and his people to enjoy an unhindered and unbroken relationship.

C. The outcome of this is seen in God's promise that no one will need to teach another because everyone, from the least to the greatest, will already know God. Contrast this with the Old Testament situation. A baby boy was circumcised when he was eight days old, when he knew nothing about God. As an adult he might rebel and never know God personally.

The final benefit of the new covenant is also the basis for its existence, forgiveness of sins. In short, God fully forgives the sins of those who accept his covenant promises by faith and thereby invites them to enjoy all the other benefits found only in the new covenant.

CONCLUSION

The new covenant established through Jesus' death on the cross both surpasses and supersedes God's old covenant with Israel. Have you signed your contract with God? If not, now is the time to sign on the dotted line. If so, then make sure that you keep your end of the bargain by serving your Lord and praising him for the benefits he has so graciously bestowed on you.

Entering God's Presence

Hebrews 9:1-10

Purpose: To experience the thrill of being able to enter the presence of God.

INTRODUCTION

Old Testament "patterns" teach us even greater ideas. For example, God's creation of the world in six days and his rest on the seventh teaches us not only about our need for rest here on earth but also about our future rest in Heaven after our work here is done (Exodus 20:11). In a similar way, God's institution of a priesthood demonstrates our need for a representative before God and allows us to see Jesus' superior priestly ministry more clearly. Likewise, the establishment of a sacrificial system teaches that death is required as atonement for sin.

The author of Hebrews also views the tabernacle (and later the temple) as a pattern of greater truth. In Hebrews 9:1-10, we learn that the tabernacle built by Moses symbolized the separation between God and his people. We can learn to appreciate our privileges as Christians by considering how much better things are for us now.

Proposition: Christ has opened up God's heavenly temple so we may have direct access to God.

I. THE TABERNACLE WAS BUILT TO RESTRICT DIRECT ACCESS TO GOD (HEBREWS 9:1-5).

A. Often when we think of the Israelite tabernacle (or temple), we get so caught up with the precious metals and religious symbols that adorned it that we fail to appreciate the layout of the building and what it signified. The tabernacle proper was surrounded by a large court where the people gathered for worship. But the people could not enter the tabernacle or temple itself.

B. The actual tabernacle consisted of two rooms, the Holy Place and the Holy of Holies (or Most Holy Place). Regular priests could enter the Holy Place as needed, but even they were prohibited from entering the Holy of Holies, the place where the ark of the covenant (where God dwelled) was kept. Only the high priest could enter the Holy of Holies, and then only once a year. Thus, one can see that the layout of the tabernacle restricted direct access to God. The tabernacle kept a sinful people at a distance from a holy God.

II. THE ISRAELITE RITUALS LIMITED PEOPLE'S PARTICIPATION IN WORSHIP (HEBREWS 9:6-10).

A. God had commanded the Israelites to perform specific rituals to atone for sin and to offer worship to him. For example, God's people were to observe feast days (Passover and Unleavened Bread, Pentecost, Tabernacles), times during which people ceased from their labors and worshiped God. The Jews were also to keep various fasts to focus their attention on God and his goodness to them.

B. Most of the Israelite rituals, however, centered around sacrifice. Every morning and night, for example, the priests sacrificed one lamb and portions of flour, oil, incense, wine, and salt (Numbers 28, 29). During the new moon sacrifices, two bulls, one ram, and seven male lambs were added to the list. Even more animals were required during the major feasts. Finally, sacrifice played an especially central role on the Day of Atonement, one day during the year when sacrifice was made for all the people's sins (Leviticus 16).

C. What is important to note about all this is the central role of the priesthood in Israel's worship. The common people were, to be sure, expected to enter into worship, but they could not perform the sacrifices or present their gifts directly to God, who was enthroned above the ark of the covenant. In sum, the Israelite rituals limited the people's participation in worship.

III. JESUS OPENED UP GOD'S TEMPLE SO WE MAY HAVE DIRECT ACCESS TO GOD.

A. When Jesus died on the cross, the veil between the Holy Place and the Holy of Holies was torn in two from top to bottom (Matthew 27:50, 51).This veil was significant. God is holy, and we are not. So there had to be a separation between us to keep us from being consumed by God's holiness. The tearing of the veil symbolized an end to the restrictions on our access to God.

B. Hebrews 10:19, 20 makes explicit what is implied in Hebrews 9, namely, that we now have direct access to the Holy of Holies, where God dwells, through the death of Jesus Christ. According to 1 Peter 2:5, we are all priests who can approach God with freedom and confidence.

CONCLUSION

Many people today regard the church platform as a holy and restricted place. In general, people feel that only "special" people such as ministers, worship leaders, or church officers should be up there.

But because of the work of Christ, we are all priests who cannot only enter God's holy places but also approach God directly. To symbolize our new access to God, we will all walk up onto the platform, then return to our seats in total silence, thanking God for the gift of free access into his presence through his Son Jesus Christ.

(Save about five to six minutes for this. Have ushers and wheelchair helpers ready to assist those who need it. Beginning at the front, have rows take turns going forward and back to their seats. Then close in prayer.)

The Blood of Christ

Hebrews 9:11-28

Purpose: To understand what the blood of Christ achieved for humanity.

INTRODUCTION

People in today's "sanitized" society often shy away from talk about or the sight of blood. Blood is, after all, often associated with pain, injury, suffering, and death. But blood plays a vital role within the Bible. The Old Testament sacrifices, for example, usually required the shedding of blood. The Israelite religion was, as it is often said, a bloody religion.

But blood is no less important for New Testament believers, for it was Jesus' shed blood that paid the penalty for our sins. Therefore, although we might cringe at the biblical emphasis on blood, we should not ignore its importance. In fact, we would do well to understand precisely what Jesus' blood accomplished for us.

Proposition: The blood of Jesus cleanses our consciences, establishes a new will, and purifies our heavenly home.

I. JESUS' BLOOD CLEANSES OUR CONSCIENCES (HEBREWS 9:11-15).

A. In the Old Testament, God taught the people the concept of separateness or holiness (being separated from ordinary things). People, foods, rituals, and places were either "clean" or "unclean." The former could participate in worship, while the latter had to be separated from anything or anyone associated with God.

Sin had rendered everything it touched unclean and thus inadmissible into God's presence. The Old Testament rituals could make it clean again, but it was always subject to defilement from sin. Physical "uncleanness" portrayed this idea constantly before the Jews.

B. The Day of Atonement was the climax of the Israelites' cleansing rituals. On that day all the people's sins were removed (Leviticus 16). But the ceremony had to be repeated every year. It did not effect a total cleansing, only a provisional removal of sin. This reminded the people that their sins were only temporarily held in abeyance. They were never fully free from them. Soon they would stumble and be guilty again.

C. Jesus' offering of his own blood totally cleansed our consciences (Hebrews 9:14). He offered himself once for all time (9:12, 13, 25-28). His sacrifice never needed to be repeated. As a result, we do not have our sins hanging over our heads. Rather, we are free to serve God with a clear conscience and a confident heart. Perhaps this is why the first words frequently heard from people who have been baptized are "I feel so clean!" Because of Jesus' blood, we are clean!

II. JESUS' BLOOD ALSO ESTABLISHED A NEW WILL (HEBREWS 9:16-22).

A. Many of us have already written our wills. In all likelihood, some have even revised their wills. When a person dies, his or her final will goes into effect. It is the same with Jesus' death. The first will (the Sinai covenant) was in effect until God changed it. Then, when Jesus died, the last will (the new covenant) went into effect.

B. Your will is not in effect now because you haven't died yet. But Jesus died on the cross, so his new will is in effect. Jesus' resurrection is proof of his power, but his death is proof that God's new will is in effect. Moreover, all those who trust in Jesus are the beneficiaries of his will and receive a good inheritance, forgiveness of sins (Hebrews 9:22). Thus, Jesus' blood not only established a new will but provided the actual benefits of that will, forgiveness of sins.

III. THE BLOOD OF JESUS PURIFIED THE HEAVENLY SANCTUARY (HEBREWS 9:23-28).

A. We often think of purification as cleaning up something that is dirty. Since God's heavenly dwelling is already pure, that is probably not what is meant here. It is best to think in Old Testament terms, where purification involved making something "clean" and available to be used in God's presence.

B. How, then, did Jesus purify the heavenly sanctuary? First, Jesus entered into God's very presence to offer his blood as a sacrifice for sin. His sacrifice was not offered in an earthly temple but in Heaven itself, in God's own presence. Moreover, Jesus offered his blood to purify those who would likewise enter into God's presence. Jesus' blood, presented as it was in the heavenly sanctuary, purified people so they could enter into God's presence without fear of punishment. We can enter God's heavenly sanctuary because Jesus' shed blood stands between us and our holy God.

CONCLUSION

In a world that demeans talk of "death on a cross" and "blood shed for our sins," it is important to recognize just what Jesus' blood accomplished for us. Jesus' blood is not something to minimize or neglect. It is, in fact, what cleanses us and enables us to receive our good inheritance (forgiveness of sins) and boldly enter into God's heavenly sanctuary and our future home. There is, after all, power in the blood. Let us never forget its wonder-working power in our lives.

Sacrificial Living

Hebrews 10:1-14

Purpose: To show how Jesus' sacrifice is superior to all other sacrifices.

INTRODUCTION

The concept of sacrifice fills the pages of the Old and New Testaments, but it doesn't always refer to the same thing. In the Old Testament, sacrifice was generally literal, the slaughter of animals or the burning of certain foods that either made atonement for sin or demonstrated one's worship of a holy God. The literal meaning of sacrifice also appears in the New Testament, but one can also observe a marked shift to a figurative use of the word. Paul, for example, regarded his life as being "poured out like a drink offering" (2 Timothy 4:6). In addition, the gift of money from Philippi was a "fragrant offering, an acceptable sacrifice, pleasing to God" (Philippians 4:18). Even Hebrews urges believers to offer the "sacrifice" of praise to God (13:15).

In light of this biblical emphasis on the importance of sacrifice, it is imperative for believers today to fully understand why Jesus' sacrifice is superior to all others and how that should affect our day to day lives as God's people.

Proposition: Jesus' finished, living, and effective sacrifice
enables us to live sacrificially for God.

I. JESUS SACRIFICED HIMSELF ONCE AND FOR ALL (HEBREWS 10:1-4).

A. The Old Testament sacrifices had to be constantly repeated. Their perpetual nature was a constant reminder of both the people's sins and the temporary status of the sacrificial system. As the author of Hebrews notes, if the sacrifices could have perfected the people, they wouldn't have been offered year after year and the people would not have "felt guilty for their sins" (Hebrews 10:2).

B. Jesus' sacrifice, however, put an end to the sacrificial system. It was offered only once for all time because it accomplished what the Old Testament sacrifices could not. It made people perfect (Hebrews 10:1) and holy (10:10). It completely cleansed any who trust in Jesus from their sins (10:4, 17, 18). As a result, it brought an end to guilt. This part is difficult for us to feel. We blame ourselves and others as though guilt remains. But Jesus freed us from our sin and its attendant guilt. Therefore, we should no longer be ruled by the sin and guilt in our lives (Romans 6:17, 18; Hebrews 10:22).

II. JESUS OFFERED HIMSELF AS A LIVING SACRIFICE (HEBREWS 10:5-10).

A. The author of Hebrews quotes Psalm 40:6-8 to make a further point, namely, that Jesus' sacrifice was "living." God always desired a devoted and obedient heart more than sacrifice (1 Samuel 15:22; Hosea 6:6). That is why the killing of animals, which did not offer themselves of their own volition, could never remove people's sins.

B. But Jesus, of his own will, offered his own body as a sacrifice for sin. The Son of God consciously chose to sacrifice his own life, thus making us holy once and for all (Hebrews 10:10). In the same way, God wants those whom Jesus has cleansed to offer themselves as living sacrifices to him (Romans 12:1, 2). It is easy for us to give things to God, but God wants our lives. Jesus gave his life, and we should do likewise.

III. JESUS' SACRIFICE WAS AN EFFECTIVE SACRIFICE (HEBREWS 10:11-14).

A. Unlike the Old Testament sacrifices, which only "worked" at achieving God's will, Jesus' sacrifice actually finished God's will. The Old Testament offerings would have stopped if they had been fully effective. Jesus' offering did stop with one offering because it was effective. Jesus' sacrifice made "perfect forever those who are being made holy" (Hebrews 10:14).

B. Therefore, we should live both sacrificially (following Jesus' example for our lives) and confidently (knowing that Jesus' effective sacrifice guarantees our perfection before the Father). Although no person could ever offer the same sacrifice as Jesus did, we can follow Jesus' example and offer our lives confidently to God because Jesus is in the process of making us perfect before the Father.

CONCLUSION

The concept of sacrifice is foreign to many people, Christians included. We live in a society that expects us to look out for our own interests, that views someone who sacrifices his or her life for others as a bit odd and foolish.

But sacrifice always has been and always will be a key part of our faith. In the first place, Jesus' sacrifice, which provides forgiveness of sins and the hope of being perfected, forms the foundation of our faith. Without Jesus' death and resurrection, we are, as Paul says, "to be pitied more than all men" (1 Corinthians 15:19). In addition, Jesus' sacrifice enables us to give ourselves as living sacrifices to God. Knowing that we have been freed from guilt and that we are in the process of being made perfect, we can follow Jesus' sacrificial model with confidence and commitment. Let us do so as we leave today and every day until Jesus returns.

Your Holiness

Hebrews 10:10

Purpose: To understand "holiness" as God and the Bible understand it.

INTRODUCTION

How would you respond if an old friend met you on the street and asked, "How are you doing, Your Holiness?" Would you think it was a joke? a subtle dig at your faith or character? Would you blush or cringe inside, recognizing how far from holy your life really is?

In reality, this question is not as farfetched as it might seem. The book of Hebrews (as well as many other biblical texts) does not hesitate to call us "holy." For example, Hebrews refers to us as holy in at least four different places:

"Both the one who makes men holy and those who are made holy are of the same family. So Jesus is not ashamed to call them brothers" (2:11).

"And by that will, we have been made holy through the sacrifice of the body of Jesus Christ once for all" (10:10).

"Because by one sacrifice he has made perfect forever those who are being made holy" (10:14).

"And so Jesus also suffered outside the city gate to make the people holy through his own blood" (13:12).

How, then, should we understand our holy status or condition? What does it mean when God refers to us as "Your Holiness"? A careful examination of God's Word will reveal what being holy is all about.

Proposition: Jesus' sacrificial death gives us a holy standing
that should be actualized in our daily lives.

I. PEOPLE ARE HOLY WHEN THEY ARE CONNECTED TO A HOLY GOD.

A. The Old Testament offers us the necessary background to understanding the idea of "holiness." Places and things were considered holy when they were set apart (or consecrated) to God's use. For example, the Holy of Holies was, in many senses, just a room, but since it was set aside as God's dwelling and throne room, it was a holy place (Hebrews 9:2, 3). Likewise, both the temple and the utensils within it became holy by their association with a holy God (Exodus 30:22-29; Acts 21:28).

B. In the same way, people become holy through their connection with a holy God. Prophets (Luke 1:70), apostles (Ephesians 3:5), elders (Titus 1:8), and even "ordinary" believers (Hebrews 3:1; 1 Peter 2:5, 9) are referred to as holy because of their special association with God. Therefore, we should neither cringe nor blush at being called "holy," for we are precisely that through our faith in Jesus Christ.

II. GOD HAS GIVEN US ALL WE NEED TO BE HOLY IN STANDING AND PRACTICE.

A. In the first place, Jesus' death removes from us the guilt and stain of sin that caused our former unholiness (Hebrews 10:10, 14; 13:12). His death and resurrection set us free from the power of sin so we can pursue a holy lifestyle (Romans 6:22). In addition, God has given us the Holy Spirit to enable us to live in a manner consistent with our standing (Romans 8:9, 10; 1 Corinthians 6:18-20).

B. God has also given us his holy Word to show us how to be holy (Romans 1:2; 2 Timothy 3:15). The Bible contains both holy laws (Romans 7:12) and holy promises (Acts 13:34) that motivate us to obedience. God also disciplines us when we fail, not out of meanness, but to prompt us to holy living (Hebrews 12:10). Because God has given us all we need for holiness, he can unhesitatingly call us to live as holy people (Romans 12:1; 2 Timothy 1:9).

III. OUR HOLY STANDING SHOULD BE ACTUALIZED IN OUR DAY-TO-DAY LIVES.

A. In light of all that God has done for us, we should pursue holiness every day of our lives. We should be set apart to God in all that we do (1 Peter 1:15, 16), cleansing ourselves of lesser purposes (2 Timothy 2:21).

B. Moreover, we should control our bodies so that they are not polluted by sin but dedicated strictly to serving God (1 Thessalonians 4:4). This will enable us to lift up holy hands in prayer to God (1 Timothy 2:8) and to purify ourselves from everything that would contaminate body or spirit (2 Corinthians 7:1). In short, we are to live holy lives (1 Thessalonians 4:7), lives that are set apart from sin and to God.

CONCLUSION

"Holiness" is, to many people, a mysterious and seemingly unattainable concept, but its meaning is not that complex. People and things become holy when they are set apart for God's exclusive use, when they are dedicated completely to God.

With regard to our own holiness, we should remind ourselves constantly that God has both made us holy and called us to holy living. God has set us apart uniquely to himself, and he expects us to live consistently with our special standing. Therefore, let us, as his holy people, purify ourselves from sin and dedicate ourselves solely to him. Then we will have no reason for shame or discomfort when someday someone refers to us as "Your Holiness."

A "Let Us" Sandwich

Hebrews 10:19-25

Purpose: To explain the different ways God nourishes us and our faith.

INTRODUCTION

This passage has a uniquely long sequence of commands beginning with the words, "Let us." In fact, its main portion has an elaborate beginning and ending, which nearly makes it a "let us" (lettuce) sandwich for Christians.

But before we get to the "insides" of the sandwich we need to know what holds it all together. The author of Hebrews offers two motivations for obedience that envelope the "lettuce" inside. The author prefaces the first motivation by writing, "Since we have confidence to enter the Most Holy Place by the blood of Jesus, by a new and living way opened for us through the curtain, that is, his body, and since we have a great priest over the house of God, let us . . ." (Hebrews 10:19-22). The second motivation is less direct but no less important. We are to obey all these commands because we know that "the Day [of Jesus' return is] approaching" (10:25).

These are strong motivations indeed. Because of what Jesus has done and will do, we should carefully consider what God would have us do.

> **Proposition:** We are nourished when we draw near to God and his hope and devote ourselves to encouraging one another to growth.

I. LET US DRAW NEAR TO GOD AND HOLD TIGHTLY TO OUR HOPE IN HIM (HEBREWS 10:21-23).

A. The first part of this "let us" sandwich involves our personal relationship to God. We are exhorted to draw near to a person, not to a religion. We should never forget that our faith is more a relationship than a set of beliefs. Thus, we should draw ever closer to God, knowing that he responds to those who approach him and "rewards those who earnestly seek him" (Hebrews 11:6).

B. We must draw near to God in sincerity, however. As in a marriage, there can be no intimate fellowship if our heart does not genuinely desire it (see John 4:23; Acts 2:46).

In addition, because Jesus has cleansed us from sin, we are to draw near to God in confidence. Like Adam and Eve, we are more likely to hide from God than to seek his presence when we sin. But God has cleansed us from a guilty conscience and washed us with pure water, so we can draw near to him in the full confidence of faith, not on account of our own ability but because of God's work on our behalf.

C. We are also encouraged to "hold unswervingly to the hope we profess." An automobile swerves, but the Greek word here speaks of bending down the head in death or in sleep, of soldiers turning in flight, and of the day declining. Thus, the idea of without relinquishing or bending seems more appropriate here. The idea is that our hold on our "hope" (or expectation) should not be loosened or relinquished because the one who promised is faithful.

II. LET US SPUR ONE ANOTHER ON TO GOOD DEEDS AND TO CORPORATE GROWTH (HEBREWS 10:24, 25).

A. When verse 24 commands us to "consider how we may spur one another on toward love and good deeds," it implies that we must plan carefully how to do this. Note that our planning does not focus on ourselves but on others. In a sense, we are to have the same attitude and concern as God, who acted on our behalf and for our good.

B. Noteworthy also is what we are to spur other Christians on toward: love and good deeds. The former is the motivating attitude (desiring the highest good for someone else), and the latter is the result (loving actions). That is, we are to encourage one another to develop loving attitudes that are demonstrated in loving actions toward other members of the church.

C. One way to "spur one another on" is by making it a "habit" to meet together. The assembled church is the best place for growth, challenge, and accountability to take place, so we dare not give it up to go our own way. Christians are responsible not only for themselves but also for each other, so they must continue to meet together to encourage one another to holy living.

CONCLUSION

As is typical in the Bible, Hebrews 10:19-25 pairs the Christian's responsibility to God with responsibility to others. Within this pairing lies a great truth, that we cannot sincerely seek God without serving others. That is why the Bible is full of "let us" passages. There are no Lone Rangers in the church. God's commands are addressed to "us."

Therefore, let us as a church commit ourselves to drawing near to God together, to holding on to our hope together, and to regularly spurring each other on to loving attitudes and good deeds. Knowing that God has already opened the way into his presence through the death of Jesus and that Jesus will someday return for his own, let us do all that we can to make sure that everyone here is ready to meet him on that grand and glorious day.

This Is Serious!

Hebrews 10:26-31

Purpose: To help people take God's specific commands for living seriously.

INTRODUCTION

A few years back a teacher was chatting with several students about the fun they were going to have just before classes started in the fall. When one student suggested, however, that it might be fun to jump on a car and hang on over the sides and fenders, the teacher's demeanor changed abruptly. This teacher had been at another campus several years before when this very kind of "fun" resulted in a freshman girl sliding off the fender and under the car, where she lost her life. Sometimes things are much more serious than we think.

Such is the perspective of Hebrews. Eugene Peterson, in *The Message*, translates the ending of Hebrews as follows: "Friends, please take what I've written most seriously" (13:22). Several passages within Hebrews reflect the author's worries about his readers. His concerns can help us avoid similar dangers.

Proposition: People can lose God's grace by embracing evil, by drifting away, or by rejecting Jesus, their only hope.

I. THOSE WHO EMBRACE EVIL WILL MISS THE GRACE OF GOD (HEBREWS 12:14-17).

A. The meaning of this and similar passages, although debated by theologians, seems clear and terribly frightening, namely, that Christians can lose God's grace. The author of Hebrews earlier referred to the people in view here as those who have been "sanctified" (10:29), which implies that even those who have experienced God's grace can lose out on its benefits.

B. To make this point, the author reminds his readers of Esau (Genesis 25:27-34). As the firstborn son, Esau held special inheritance rights, but he traded those rights for a single meal. As Hebrews states, Esau could not bring about a change of mind, "though he sought the blessing with tears" (12:17). He had made his choice and had to live with the consequences of that choice. In the same way, those who prefer evil to God's grace must live with their choice.

C. This tragic fate can be avoided, however. Instead of choosing evil, we should make every effort to live in peace with others and to live holy lives (Hebrews 12:14), avoid all traces of bitterness that trouble and defile many (12:15), and keep ourselves from immorality and godlessness (12:16). We must, above all, focus our attention on God's grace (his forgiveness of our sins) and enablement for righteous living.

II. THOSE WHO DRIFT AWAY FROM JESUS WILL EXPERIENCE THE PUNISHMENT OF GOD (HEBREWS 2:1-4; 6:4-12).

A. According to Hebrews 2:1-4, Christians drift away by not paying close attention to the message that they have heard. In earlier days, inattention to the covenant at Mount Sinai brought full and just punishment. Now that Jesus has brought a superior covenant, failure to pay close attention will bring an even greater punishment.

B. Hebrews 6:4-12 adds that such "drifting" may be a sign of spiritual laziness. It is not sufficient simply to see and experience God's mighty power (6:4, 5). We must also be diligent to make our hope sure (6:11, 12). Otherwise, we are no better than unproductive land that soaks in the rain without producing a crop, worthless land in danger of being cursed and burned (6:7, 8). Drifting away from Jesus is a serious matter, for it leads to nothing less than eternal punishment.

III. THOSE WHO CONTINUE IN SIN WILL FACE THE WRATH OF GOD (HEBREWS 10:26-31).

A. Sin is quite possibly the most insidious (and serious) danger that Hebrews takes time to address. Most professing Christians would never consciously choose evil (Hebrews 12:14-17) or "drift" from their commitment to Jesus as Savior. But, as Paul observed in Romans, some use God's grace as an excuse to sin (6:1-14).

B. Such an attitude is a grave error and a serious danger. It is nothing less than trampling "the Son of God under foot," than treating "as an unholy thing the blood of the covenant," than insulting "the Spirit of grace" (Hebrews 10:29). There is "no sacrifice for sins" for such a one but only "a fearful expectation of judgment and of raging fire that will consume the enemies of God" (10:26, 27). God's wrath, even on "his people," on those who have been "sanctified," (10:30, 29), is both real and "dreadful" (10:31). Therefore, let us never reject the truth we have received by deliberately continuing in sin (10:26, 28).

CONCLUSION:

There are a million different ways to miss God's grace, but only one way to enjoy it now and throughout eternity. Only faith in and obedience to Jesus our Savior will deliver us from the dreadful judgment that awaits "the enemies of God" (Hebrews 10:27). The dangers of choosing evil or drifting away from our commitment to Jesus may not be great in a group such as this, but the tendency to continue in sin poses a serious and ongoing threat. Let us be sure that we never trample Jesus under foot and place ourselves in danger of God's wrath by continuing in deliberate sin. Sin is, after all, serious business indeed.

An "Effective" Faith

Hebrews 11:1-7

Purpose: To discover some of the many practical effects of faith in God.

INTRODUCTION

Every aspect of life operates on the principle of faith. For example, we make business deals because we believe in someone else's truthfulness. In the same way, we trust that only safe water will come from a faucet or drinking fountain and that the gasoline that powers our cars will not blow us up. Even non-Christians who claim to be "beyond faith" still trust in their own ability to decide what is true.

So it is hard to understand why some people today want to devalue faith and elevate some other standard by which to live. The truth is, faith is as vital a part of our lives as breathing, eating, and sleeping. So as Christians we should not be ashamed about having faith. Rather, we should rejoice that God uses such an effective means to draw us closer to him. Hebrews 11:1-7 can help us do that by identifying some of the good effects that faith in God produces.

Proposition: Faith affects the way we understand our world, worship God, live our lives, and face death.

I. FAITH INFLUENCES THE WAY WE UNDERSTAND OUR WORLD (HEBREWS 11:3).

A. Faith in God helps one understand that God formed the world by his word. Genesis 1 repeats numerous times that God said, "Let there be . . ." and that whatever God commanded came into existence (see also Psalm 33:6-9). The universe is so complex that it cannot have arisen just by chance.

B. Today many evolutionists reject the biblical claim, contending that the "hard facts of science" must replace religious belief. But evolution is not a scientific experiment that can be repeated, so it too must depend on the faith of its adherents.

C. Belief in a God who created all that exists, however, provides the possibility and the rationale for exploring our world. Through God's creation we learn not only about God's awesome power but also about his care for the tiniest details (see Romans 1:20). In the final analysis, faith is not an impediment to our understanding. On the contrary, faith helps us to understand the world as God intended.

II. FAITH AFFECTS THE WAY WE WORSHIP GOD (HEBREWS 11:4).

A. Hebrews 11:4 clears up what has long been a perplexing question: Why did God accept Abel's sacrifice but not Cain's? Some have argued that the difference in what they offered (lambs as opposed to grain products) determined God's response, but both were acceptable offerings later in Israel's history. In reality, the difference was not in *what* they offered but in *how* it was offered. Abel offered a sacrifice in faith; Cain did not.

B. The lesson for us should be obvious. For our worship to be acceptable, we must come to God in faith, praising him because we believe him worthy of praise and praying to him because we believe he hears and answers. Instead of merely going through the motions of "worship actions," we are to worship God in spirit and in truth (John 4:23), the two components of a genuine faith.

III. FAITH AFFECTS HOW WE LIVE OUR LIVES AND FACE DEATH (HEBREWS 11:5-7).

A. Hebrews 11:7 holds up for us to consider the example of Noah. This man of God had never seen a flood like the one about to come, but he believed God enough to begin the time-consuming project of building a massive boat. We do not know how long Noah worked on the ark, but it is likely that he spent many years devoted to this one task (Genesis 6:13-17; 1 Peter 3:20).

B. Today's reactions are built on what we expect will happen tomorrow. Noah had only God's word about tomorrow, but that was enough. In holy fear he worked without ceasing until God's task was done. Noah's faith shaped how he lived each day, and it should do no less for us today.

C. Enoch, on the other hand, demonstrates how faith should influence the way we face death. Hebrews 11:5, 6 (citing Genesis 5:21-24) reminds us that faith enables us to escape the fear of death. Enoch trusted God, so God rewarded him by taking him to his heavenly reward. If we, like Enoch, believe that God exists and that he rewards those who earnestly seek him (Hebrews 11:6), we too can face death with the confident expectation that it is but our final step into God's presence.

CONCLUSION

Contrary to popular opinion, faith is perhaps the highest "achievement" anyone can attain. Although many people today, Christians and non-Christians alike, seem to believe that knowledge or power or money is greater than faith, nothing could be further from the truth.

Faith is not only our greatest privilege but also the means by which we can understand our world, worship God in a way that pleases him, conduct our lives in a productive manner, and face the fear of inevitable death. Faith is the one effective force in our lives. Let us never cease to live by faith or forget to thank God for giving to us such a great gift.

A Remarkable Faith

Hebrews 11:8-19

Purpose: To see how God does impossible things for and through believers.

INTRODUCTION

Abraham was as human as the rest of us. Like us, he awoke every morning to face a world filled with possibility and peril. Abraham did his work, he ate his meals, and every night he lay down to sleep, only to get up the next morning to repeat his routine all over again. Indeed, Abraham, that great hero of the Old Testament, was very much like us.

But Abraham *was* a hero. Today, nearly four thousand years after Abraham lived on this earth, we still remember his name and the great deeds he accomplished for God. What set apart this most ordinary of men? Why does the Bible remember him as one whose example we should follow? Hebrews 11 explains how God did remarkable things through this unremarkable man.

> **Proposition:** God accomplishes extraordinary things through ordinary people when they have faith.

I. BY FAITH ABRAHAM LEFT HIS HOME AND WENT TO A FARAWAY LAND (HEBREWS 11:8-10).

A. Abraham's remarkable deeds began with a divine call (Hebrews 11:8). In the same way, if we are to achieve something significant for God, we must begin with God's initiative, not our own. God calls each of us to special tasks, so we must listen carefully for what God would have *us* do. God did not call others of Abraham's day to leave their countries for a distant land, but that does not mean God did not have a calling for their lives. Different people are called in different ways, and each must do what God requires.

For example, three times Oswald Smith tried to go to a mission field. Three times he had to return. So he concluded that, if he could not go himself, he would send others. Eventually his congregation grew in missions giving until they were sending $7 away for every $1 they used at home. At one point they supported three hundred missionaries by themselves. Some are called to go, some to work at home. Abraham was called to go.

B. What makes Abraham so remarkable is not his calling but his obedient faith. Abraham did not even know where he was going. He knew only that God had promised to give him a new land as an inheritance and that the God who can be trusted must also be obeyed. So Abraham made a home in this new land, though it would be four hundred years before his descendants would own it. Abraham lived in tents as a stranger there, but he never lost faith in God or the promise he had received (Hebrews 7:9). By faith Abraham obeyed God's calling for his life. By faith we can do the same.

II. BY FAITH ABRAHAM BECAME A FATHER WHEN HE WAS TOO OLD TO DO SO (HEBREWS 11:11-16).

A. Abraham was plainly too old to father a child, and Sarah was equally beyond the age of childbearing. But as he often does, God promised the impossible and expected his people to respond in faith. And when Abraham and Sarah did what was humanly ridiculous, God made the impossible happen!

B. Abraham could have looked at the situation and concluded that it was all a misunderstanding, that God did not expect him to believe in an impossible dream. But Abraham kept his faith in the face of impossible odds, and God gave him not only a son (Hebrews 11:11) but also innumerable descendants and a heavenly home (11:12, 16). By faith Abraham experienced God's ability to achieve the impossible. By faith we can experience the same.

III. BY FAITH ABRAHAM REASONED THAT GOD COULD RAISE THE DEAD (HEBREWS 11:17-19).

A. God's promise to give Abraham many children through Isaac conflicted with his command to sacrifice Isaac, yet Abraham obeyed without hesitation. As one writer remarks, "With destiny before him and Isaac at his side, Abraham set out for the mountain." Abraham's thought process could be represented as follows:

Fact 1: God promised me many descendants through Isaac.
Fact 2: God has now commanded me to put Isaac to death.
Conclusion: To keep his promise, God will raise Isaac from the dead.

B. What is important to see here is that Abraham did not use God's promise as an excuse to disobey. Neither did he argue with God, trying to point out the apparent conflict between the promise and the command. Rather, Abraham trusted God to keep his promise and obeyed even when it might appear that doing so would bring an end to that very promise. By faith Abraham obeyed God in the face of an "impossible" command. By faith we can do the same.

CONCLUSION

Abraham was a remarkable man, not because of his gifts or abilities, his wealth or his power, but simply because he lived by faith. God may not call you or test you as he did this hero of faith, but he does want you to obediently trust him to do impossible things for him.

How far will your faith lead you? Can it lead you to reach a faraway country? to go beyond your ability and to achieve an impossible dream? to obey God even when it might cost you everything? What can God do with you and your faith?

One Car, Many Drivers

Hebrews 11:23-28

Purpose: To see how faith is the same, but each person's application of it is unique.

INTRODUCTION

One of the errors that believers frequently fall into is assuming that God works the same in everyone's life. For example, those with a passion for evangelism sometimes grow frustrated with those who focus on other needs. Similarly, at times Christians who experience God's presence with a particular type of worship have a hard time accepting those with different tastes.

But just as the same car can go slow or fast, down one road or another, depending on the driver, so faith in different people leads them to do different things. God does not lead us all down exactly the same road, although we are all ultimately headed in the same direction. Nowhere is this more evident than in the life of Moses.

Proposition: Moses' faith in God led him in unusual directions, and our faith in God may require us to do the same.

I. MOSES' FAITH BEGAN WHEN HIS PARENTS HID HIM TO SAVE HIS LIFE (HEBREWS 11:23).

A. Moses was born in an unusually perilous time, and his life was in danger the moment he took his first breath (see Exodus 1:8–2:2). One might regard this as a portent for the unusual course his life was to take.

B. But Moses' parents, being people of faith, could see that "he was no ordinary child, and they were not afraid of the king's edict," so they hid him for three months after he was born (Hebrews 11:23). This act, which could have cost them their lives, demonstrates great faith in God, and it is not too difficult to imagine that this one act of faith shaped how their unusual son viewed both his life and his relationship with God. By faith Moses' parents defied a cruel command and changed the course of history for their son and their people. By faith parents today can influence their children in a similar way.

II. MOSES' FAITH LED HIM TO CHOOSE THE PERMANENT OVER THE PLEASANT (HEBREWS 11:24-26).

A. Few people would trade position and power for a place among the despised of this world—but that is exactly what Moses did. In his case faith demanded that he give up the trappings and advantages of a royal court to suffer mistreatment alongside God's people. According to Hebrews, he did this because "he regarded disgrace for the sake of Christ as of greater value than the treasures of Egypt, because he was looking ahead to his reward" (11:26).

B. God may not ask us to do what Moses did—Joseph, for example, served God by staying in Pharaoh's court—but he always wants us to take the long view. People of faith reject the transitory in favor of the permanent, give up what is pleasurable when it conflicts with God's leading in their lives.

III. MOSES' FAITH MOVED HIM TO CHOOSE FLIGHT OVER FIGHT (HEBREWS 11:27).

A. Sometimes God calls us to stand courageously as we fight the good fight. On other occasions God asks to flee the battle. One might think that faith would always fight, but this is not the case. Hebrews explains that Moses fled Egypt because of his faith in God (11:27). Moses was not worried that fleeing might somehow sidetrack God's plans for his life. He simply followed the leading of his "invisible" God.

B. This was also Jesus' choice in Matthew 12. Incensed that Jesus had healed a man on the Sabbath, the Pharisees plotted how they might kill him. Instead of fighting or resisting their threats, Jesus simply withdrew. Jesus and Moses recognized that sometimes it takes greater faith to flee than it does to stand and fight. God will accomplish his purposes, so his people should faithfully obey whether he calls them to flee or to fight.

IV. MOSES' FAITH MOTIVATED HIM TO OBEY AN UNUSUAL COMMAND (HEBREWS 11:28).

A. God's instructions concerning the Passover (Exodus 12) must have sounded odd when Moses first heard them. Never before had the Israelites celebrated a feast such as this, and one had to wonder how smearing blood on the door-posts, not breaking any bones of the lambs, and staying indoors would keep them alive. But Moses showed great faith by obeying even this unusual command, and in the process protected God's people from certain death.

B. We are no longer obligated to observe the Passover, but God likewise asks us to do unusual things, such as not retaliate, give to anyone who asks from us, subordinate our interests to the interests of others, reject our families for the sake of Christ, and forgive those who hurt us again and again. If, like Moses, we are people of true faith, we will obey God's directions no matter how odd they seem to be.

CONCLUSION

God is calling each of us to faith, but that does not mean that faith will lead all of us in the same direction. Faith might lead some of you to a far-off land, while faith might lead others to minister to the poor among us. The real question is not where faith is leading your neighbor. Rather, where is your faith leading you?

A Little Faith Does a Lot

Hebrews 11:31-39

Purpose: To retell the story of Rahab to discover the nature of risk-taking faith.

INTRODUCTION

People of all ages are fascinated by tales of heroic battles and courageous deeds. Similarly, as a wide-eyed little girl, Rahab must have heard stories about the ten plagues, Israel crossing the Red Sea, and the destruction of Egypt's army.

But that was forty years ago. Now she heard fresh stories about the powerful Amorite kings, Sihon and Og, whom Israel had utterly destroyed east of the Jordan River. The swollen Jordan could only keep Israel away for a little while longer.

Proposition: Rahab's tiny faith led her to seize great opportunities.

I. BY FAITH RAHAB SEIZED THE OPPORTUNITY TO KNOW GOD.

A. Rahab's inn provided constant contact with travelers. It was a useful place to add current information to childhood stories about Israel and their God. She learned that the Israelite laws were different. There could be no adultery—no satisfying of the natural hungers of men. Every seventh day they did no work at all. Swift punishment paralleled the crime but required two witnesses.

B. The Israelite God was different. He was bigger than other gods. Israel said he had created everything. Rahab was familiar with local gods. People in Jericho worshiped many gods but gave special prominence to the moon god. The Israelite God seemed to be a God of love, but far different from the goddess of love widely worshiped in Canaan. He was certainly powerful but also gentle and protective.

The Israelite God was also true. Merchants had heard the Israelites talking about promises their God had made hundreds of years before, promises he was now keeping. The gods Rahab knew were very capricious, quite unpredictable. Sometimes she wondered if the nature of the gods was not simply invented by the priests to get what they wanted. But such thoughts sounded heretical, and she never even whispered them to her nearest friends.

C. Rahab was intrigued by the different customs and superstitions she saw in travelers from many cultures. But this group was different, even fascinating. Above all, she was captivated by their God. She wondered what it would be like to be a woman among these people, a woman respected.

55

II. BY FAITH RAHAB SEIZED THE OPPORTUNITY TO DECIDE.

A. Now the Israelites were poised on the East bank of the swollen Jordan. They were evidently going to cross when the water receded. They had been wandering the southern desert for forty years, but in the last few months they had rounded Edom, south of the Dead Sea, and defeated the two powerful Amorite kings, Sihon and Og. Who could stop them?

B. Suddenly it happened. Two men appeared at her inn wearing distinctively Israelite clothing. What would she do? If she reported them to the king of Jericho, she would be hailed as a hero. For what? If she helped them, perhaps she could somehow join them and their God.

C. It did not take long for her to decide. She offered them protection. The king's watchmen had also noted the peculiar dress and reported their presence to the king. Rahab warned the men that they must hide immediately. Then she pointed the king's men another way. When she was able to return to them, she reported that the people of Jericho were terrified because of the reports of what "the LORD your God, God in heaven above and on the earth below" had done. She requested two things—an oath and a sign. Then, the next day she hurried them safely away.

D. She did not know this opportunity would arise. But when it came she acted very quickly on the tiny bits of information she had gathered and pondered.

III. BY FAITH RAHAB SEIZED THE CHANCE TO BE REWARDED.

A. When Jericho melted in fear at the news that the Israelites had miraculously crossed the Jordan, Rahab breathed an excited prayer of anticipation to this new God up there. "They are coming, God. Please protect me and my family in whatever happens."

B. The warriors of Jericho were so engrossed in the Israelite approach and strange marching around the wall that no one noticed all of Rahab's relatives waiting with her at her house. Rahab had nothing but an opportunity, but her faith led her to risk and rescue not only her own life but also the lives of her family.

CONCLUSION

Bibles were scarce during the Communist oppression in Russia. I once read of a man in Eastern Russia who felt that if he could somehow get to Moscow he would be able to get a Bible in Red Square. After traveling three thousand miles, he "happened" to arrive at the Square just as a Bible peddler show up, and they "happened" to find one another. He got his Bible and returned home.

In what direction is faith leading you? Is God giving you an opportunity to know him? to decide for him? to be rewarded by him? Risk all, and succeed like Rahab.

Run for Your Life!

Hebrews 12:1-3

Purpose: To be encouraged to persevere to the very end, as others have done.

INTRODUCTION

Few moments in sports are more thrilling than watching our hero round the last turn, catch the approving roar from the stands, and lean forward into the winning tape. There is something about watching a good race that causes our blood to surge and makes us want to stand up and cheer.

Perhaps that is why the Bible compares the Christian life to a thrilling race. Those who run undergo the rigors of training in order to attain greater rewards, and so it is with the Christian life. Hebrews 12:1-3 spells out just how the Christian life is like a race and tells us how we should run "the race marked out for us" (12:1).

Proposition: As those who seek to win God's prize, we should run wisely and diligently to the end.

I. AS IN A RACE, WE ARE SURROUNDED BY MANY WITNESSES (HEBREWS 12:1a, 2).

A. Perhaps you have witnessed one of those rare occasions when the first ones to finish a long race stand along the sidelines and cheer the others along to finish the race. So it is with our Christian faith. The Old Testament believers whose faith was recounted in Hebrews 11 are presented in 12:1 as spectators watching our progress in the faith.

B. Although this image may strike some as odd, it is consistent with the notion that we are all members of the same body and that every member is to help the others (1 Corinthians 12:13, 24b, 25). Therefore, it does not seem too far-fetched to suggest that all of God's saints from ages past are cheering us on as we press toward the finish line.

C. Of course, Christians today have an even greater body of witnesses than the original readers of Hebrews. In addition to the Old Testament saints listed in Hebrews 11, we also have the example and encouragement of believers who have finished their race since then. Our witnesses include Christians such as Paul and Barnabas, Stephen and Timothy, pillars of the first-century church. Also present are John Huss, a fourteenth-century preacher who was burned at the stake, and Martin Luther, the principle voice of the Reformation. But let us not forget that watchful elder, patient teacher, or committed preacher who helped shape our faith years ago. Above all, let us not lose sight of Jesus, "the author and perfecter of our faith" (Hebrews 12:2), who finished his race so that we might do the same.

II. WE MUST RUN WISELY BY THROWING OFF ANYTHING THAT WEIGHTS US DOWN (HEBREWS 12:1b).

A. Just as a runner would never compete wearing a heavy uniform, Christians must make sure that they are not weighted down with unnecessary baggage. It is all too easy for us to become attached to the things of this world (1 John 2:15, 16), so we must constantly throw off those things that slow us down.

B. The author of Hebrews mentions two types of impediments that hinder our progress. The first type is not overtly sinful, but it "hinders" us just the same. In reality, "good" things such as work, recreation, money, and friends often become the enemy of the best and keep us from running as effectively as we could. We must "throw off" even the good things if they hinder our progress in our Christian faith.

The second type of impediment (sin) is often more destructive than the first. Lust dilutes our devotion, while immorality destroys our witness. Pride creates divisions within the body, while gossip destroys the body from within. A quick temper drives others away from us, while hypocrisy drives them away from Christ. All these sins and others, which entangle us all too easily, must be thrown off if we are to run the race of the Christian life.

III. WE MUST RUN DILIGENTLY TO THE END EVEN IF WE BECOME EXHAUSTED (HEBREWS 12:1c, 3).

A. What really matters is not how we begin the Christian life but how we end it. As Jesus taught in the parable of the soils, the only reliable evidence of faith is the production of fruit. Yet who among us has not felt the temptation to ease up when we grow tired of living the Christian life? We all become weary from opposition and the difficult work of Christian living. Yet God exhorts us not to give up.

B. Like Jesus, we should focus on the joy that awaits us instead of the struggles that we presently face. Jesus encountered far greater opposition than we will ever face, so we must follow his example and run diligently to the end. If we do, we will receive a great reward that long outlasts our current weariness.

CONCLUSION

The Christian life is, in many ways, both a thrilling race and a grueling struggle. It should comfort us to know that others have gone before us and even now stand on the sidelines cheering us on. Like them, we can finish our race successfully and win the prize (eternal life) that God has promised those who run well. Yet in order to do this we must run wisely and diligently, setting aside everything that slows us down as we doggedly press on toward the finish line that lies ahead.

The Hard Part of Living

Hebrews 12:3-13

Purpose: To understand that God disciplines us because he loves us.

INTRODUCTION

God never promised that our lives would be easy and pleasant. Indeed, Job 14:1, which says that "Man born of woman is of few days and full of trouble," seems to capture the nature of life more accurately than we might want to admit. Difficulties come from different sources: from ourselves, from others, from nature, from Satan, and even from God.

What sets Christians apart is not our immunity from difficulty but in the way that we respond to difficulty when it arises. Instead of viewing hardship as a threatening evil, we are to regard it as discipline and training from God. Just as a coach pushes athletes during practice to help them perform when it really counts, so God allows us to struggle and suffer today so we will be ready to meet him when Jesus returns. In this vein, Hebrews 12:3-13 tells us how to deal with difficulties when they arise.

Proposition: God uses hardships to train us for life,
so we must endure them with the proper attitude.

I. WE SHOULD CONSIDER OTHERS WHO HAVE FACED SUFFERING (HEBREWS 12:3).

A. Making the most of God's training begins with developing the right attitude toward the hardships we face. We are not the first to struggle, and we will not be the last. Instead of falling into the pit of self-pity, we must recognize that we are but facing what others have faced.

B. Jesus, for example, suffered greatly through no fault of his own. Although he was without sin, he was blindfolded, struck with fists and a stick, abandoned by his closest friends, insulted, slapped, taunted, mocked, wrongly accused, spit upon, and crucified. Jesus underwent all this and so "learned obedience from what he suffered" (Hebrews 5:8). Jesus focused on the joy set before him instead of his suffering (12:3). Therefore, we should consider what Jesus suffered when we face troubles and follow his example to the very end.

II. WE MUST REMEMBER THAT GOD DISCIPLINES THE ONES HE LOVES (HEBREWS 12:4-11).

A. The word "discipline" has an ominous ring to it, calling to mind punishment for sin or some wrongdoing. The notion of punishment is in view here, but it is not the entire picture, for the author makes no mention of sin. That is why the word "train" is a better choice in this context. God uses the hardships of this world to discipline us when we sin *and* to train us in holiness (Hebrews 12:10).

B. What is more important to remember is that God disciplines and trains only those whom he loves, only those who are members of his family (Hebrews 12:6, 7). Just as a parent disciplines a child out of a love that seeks the child's highest good, so God trains us through the struggles of life because he loves us and wants what is best for us (12:9, 10). That is why, although discipline is painful for a moment, it is far better than the alternative, not to be a genuine child of God (12:8). God's discipline and training lead us to life (12:9), are for our good (12:10), enable us to share in God's holiness (12:10), and produce in us a harvest pleasing to God (12:11).

C. So when we undergo hardships and difficulties, we should endure them with an open and teachable heart, actively remembering that our God uses even the hard and painful aspects of life to produce in us "a harvest of righteousness and peace" (Hebrews 12:11). Like professional athletes, we must endure the necessary training so we can perform at peak level when the game is on the line.

III. WE MUST STRENGTHEN OURSELVES AND OTHERS TO ENDURE DIFFICULTIES (HEBREWS 12:7, 12, 13).

A. Christianity is not for the weak or the easily wearied. It takes strength of will and character to keep one's faith in the face of opposition. We cannot escape difficulties in this life, but we can overcome them if we strengthen ourselves to face the battle.

B. But we must not focus so much on strengthening ourselves that we neglect the weak among us who need help and healing (Hebrews 12:13). We are, it is true, to endure hardship as good soldiers of Jesus (2 Timothy 2:3), but we are also called to endure the hardships of others (Galatians 6:2). As members of the same team, we must work for the good (and the victory) of the whole. In sum, we must strengthen both ourselves and others so we can all endure the difficulties we will inevitably face and win the prize God promises those who persevere.

CONCLUSION

God never promised to keep us from life's storms, but he will give us safe passage to our heavenly port. In fact, God uses the storms to train us to be more like Christ, who likewise learned obedience through the things he suffered. Knowing this, let us strengthen ourselves to face the battle, brace ourselves to endure unto the end. Let us never forget the hope that lies before us. Let us never give up. Let us never give in.

Come to This Mountain

Hebrews 12:18-29

Purpose: To contrast the Old Testament with the New by the image of two mountains.

INTRODUCTION

There is something about mountains that lifts the human heart and calls us upward to scale their heights. Mountain climbers, for example, are drawn to majestic peaks by a pull that is almost beyond their control. A few even risk life and limb to summit ice-capped peaks simply "because they are there."

Christians likewise speak of "mountaintop" experiences, times when they scale the spiritual heights to encounter God in a particularly moving way. This should not be surprising, for God has used mountains throughout history to teach his people key lessons and to call them ever higher in their walk with him. Hebrews 12:18-29 even uses the imagery of mountains to show us how much higher our spiritual calling is than God's earlier calling of the Israelite people.

Proposition: God has called us to his heavenly mountain, so we must not settle for the lower elevations.

I. GOD CALLED ISRAEL FROM THE HEIGHTS OF MOUNT SINAI (HEBREWS 12:18-21).

A. The scene alluded to in these verses is described in full in Exodus 19 and 20. When Israel approached "the mountain of God," there was thunder and lightning, a thick cloud over the top of the mountain, and the ringing of a loud trumpet blast. Everyone in the camp trembled. Mount Sinai was covered with fire and smoke that billowed up like smoke from a furnace. The entire mountain trembled violently. When the people heard the thunder and saw the lightning, they trembled with fear and stayed at a distance.

B. This terrifying scene was designed to test the people so that the fear of God would keep them from sinning (Exodus 20:20). God planned to make Israel his special people, a holy nation. Exodus 19:5 and 6 explains, "If you obey me fully and keep my covenant, then out of all nations you will be my treasured possession. Although the whole earth is mine, you will be for me a kingdom of priests and a holy nation" (see also Deuteronomy 14:2; 26:18, 19).

C. God's call at Sinai was frightening, but some Israelites rejected God in spite of what they had seen and heard. As the author of Hebrews notes, those who did so did not escape God's consuming wrath (12:26). When God calls from a mountain, his people must listen and obey.

II. GOD CALLS NEW ISRAEL, THE CHURCH, FROM HIS HEAVENLY MOUNTAIN (HEBREWS 12:22-24).

A. Hebrews 12:22 states that we have come to Mount Zion, which was the seat of God's temple and the center of Old Testament religion. But the mountain from which God calls us is no earthly heap of rocks. It is the "heavenly" city of our "living God." The Israelites encountered God at a physical mountain, but we are called even higher.

B. In addition, whereas the Israelites "met" God indirectly through the smoke, fire, and trumpet blast, we "have come to God" himself through the finished work of Jesus (Hebrews 12:23). It is important to note the contrast between the phenomena that accompany each encounter. The Israelites experienced "darkness, gloom and storm" and "a voice speaking" (12:18, 19). Christians, however, enjoy the company of "thousands upon thousands of angels," "the church of the firstborn," "the spirits of righteous men," God our Father, and Jesus our Savior (12:22-24). In every way God's call to his new people from his holy mountain surpasses the earlier call to Israel from Mount Sinai.

III. WE MUST NOT IGNORE OR REFUSE GOD'S CALL FOR US TO BE HOLY (HEBREWS 12:25-28).

A. Just as God called Israel to be a holy people, so he calls us to holy living that will enable us to see him (Hebrews 12:14). "Holiness" is not some mystical concept but the ethical purity that results from separating oneself from the world and to God. It requires living at peace with others, keeping pure from sexual immorality, and avoiding bitterness and other destructive attitudes (12:14-16).

B. God's grace to us should be enough to motivate us to holiness, but if it is not we should at least recall the Israelite experience. Those who reject God's call will still encounter God, but only as "a consuming fire" (Hebrews 12:29). God promises to give us a kingdom that cannot be shaken (12:28), but if we reject it we will be shaken to our very souls.

CONCLUSION

God calls us to a "mountaintop experience," to a spiritual height on which we can rest secure. God calls us to his heavenly mountain where we can enjoy the company of not only saints and angels but also God himself.

Still, we must not forget that God's heavenly mountain is also his holy mountain. In order to achieve the heights to which God has called us, we must be sure that we neither ignore nor reject his high calling. Only the holy will see God, so let us scale the heights God has set before us by trusting in Jesus' sacrifice for our sins and then responding to his finished work through holy living.

Christ in My Neighbor

Hebrews 13:1-9

Purpose: To learn to serve others as though each were Jesus himself.

INTRODUCTION

Harriet Richie tells a story about looking for a restaurant after a Christmas Eve service. Nothing was open but an unholy smelling truck stop. Harriet felt uncomfortable when she noted that the only people present were a wisp-thin waitress and a one-armed man sitting at the counter. Then a young couple arrived. When their tiny baby began to cry, the waitress offered to hold him a while, and the one-armed man whistled and made silly faces until the baby stopped crying. Later, when Harriet and her husband walked out the door, Harriet's husband reminded her that the angel had said, "I bring good news of great joy to *all* people." Harriet realized that Jesus would probably have headed straight for this place.

It is easy for Christians to overlook certain people when we consider whom Jesus wants us to care about. Yet Jesus himself told us that the way we treat others is how we treat him (Matthew 25:34-45). The final chapter of Hebrews reminds us that we must not only see but serve Christ in our neighbors.

Proposition: When we show love to others, we give love to our Lord.

I. LOVE INVOLVES DETECTING AND MEETING OTHERS' NEEDS (HEBREWS 13:1-3).

A. As Paul wrote in 1 Corinthians 8:1, "Knowledge puffs up, but love builds up." It is not enough to know about others and their needs. We must also reach out to them in love. All too often those in the Christian community discuss fellow believers and their troubles under the guise of learning "how to pray for them more effectively." In reality, we don't need to know about others so much as we need to serve them in love.

B. Also, we are to love all people without discrimination. As Jesus taught in the parable of the good Samaritan, anyone with a need that we can meet is our neighbor (Luke 10:25-37), but our love should be especially directed toward those who are our "brothers" in the faith (Hebrews 13:1; Galatians 6:10).

C. By way of illustration, Hebrews 13:2, 3 tells us to detect and meet the needs of two types of people: strangers and prisoners. Jews were to give strangers special help, since they knew what it was to be strangers in someone else's land (Exodus 23:9). We as Christians should also understand this, since we are strangers in this world (1 Peter 2:11). In fact, by entertaining strangers, some people have entertained angels without knowing it (see Genesis 18). We are also to "remember" those in prison (Hebrews 13:3), putting ourselves in their place and doing for them what we would want others to do for us. In other words, we are to show active love to others even when they are unable to return the favor. Love does not count the cost. Rather, it detects the need and meets that need without any thought of reward.

II. LOVE REQUIRES US TO HONOR THE GIFTS GOD HAS GIVEN US (HEBREWS 13:4-6).

A. Sometimes in looking after the needs of others, we lose sight of what is truly important. For example, we should not love others to the neglect of a spouse (Hebrews 13:2). Marriage is a marvelous gift from God, so we must honor it by keeping it pure. This means, of course, that we should keep the "marriage bed" pure from sexual immorality, but it also involves honoring our spouse through loving actions and attitudes. God established marriage as a place of communion, and he expects his people to honor it as such.

B. On the other hand, we should not "honor" money so highly that we become dissatisfied with what God has given us. It is far better to be without money and have God than to be without God and have money (Hebrews 13:5). God will give us all that we need, so we should keep ourselves free from the love of money and be content with what we have (13:5, 6).

III. LOVE MOTIVATES US TO ACTIVELY REMEMBER THOSE WHO LEAD US (HEBREWS 13:7, 8).

A. We can "remember" those who lead us in various ways: by praying for them, by encouraging them, and also by supporting them financially. Galatians 6:6 explains, "Anyone who receives instruction in the word must share all good things with his instructor."

B. Another way to "remember" our leaders is by considering their example. It is said that imitation is highest form of compliment, so by copying our leaders' example of following our unchanging Lord we give them our highest praise (Hebrews 13:7, 8). We show love to them (and to Jesus) by submitting to their guidance and journeying with them along the pathway of faith.

CONCLUSION

There can be no love of God without a corresponding love for people. That is why Jesus taught that our acts of love to others are actually done to him. If we genuinely love God, we will detect and meet the needs of those he brings our way, honor the gifts God has given us in a way that honors him, and remember those he has given us to lead us in our walk with him.

Jesus came to love and serve others. Do we love him enough to do the same?